D0938780

STARS IN THE CORPS

From the Same Authors

*Shooting the War: The Memoir and Photographs
of a U-Boat Officer in World War II,* 1994
Otto Geise and James E. Wise, Jr.

Stars in Blue: Movie Actors in America's Sea Services, 1997
James E. Wise, Jr., and Anne Collier Rehill

*Stars in Khaki: Movie Actors in the U.S. Army
and Army Air Corps*
James E. Wise, Jr., and Paul Wilderson
Forthcoming

STARS IN THE CORPS

Movie Actors in the United States Marines

James E. Wise, Jr., and Anne Collier Rehill

NAVAL INSTITUTE PRESS
Annapolis, Maryland

Library of Congress Cataloging-in-Publication Data
Wise, James E., 1930–
   Stars in the corps : movie actors in the United States Marines / James E. Wise, Jr. and Anne Collier Rehill.
      p.   cm.
   Includes bibliographical references and index.
   ISBN 1-55750-949-2 (alk. paper)
   1. Motion picture actors and actresses—United States—Biography. 2. Motion pictures—United States—Biography. 3. United States. Marine Corps—Biography.   I. Rehill, Anne Collier, 1950– .
II. Title.
PN1998.2.W56   1999
791.43'028'0973—dc21
[B]   99-11917

Printed in the United States of America on acid-free paper ⊗

06 05 04 03 02 01 00 99   9 8 7 6 5 4 3 2
First printing

Unless otherwise noted, all photographs are from the U.S. Marine Corps.

For Anne's parents, Barbara and Clayton Collier
and for Jim's sons, Jim III and Matt

Contents

Appendixes

Preface

Semper Fidelis, "always faithful," has been the U.S. Marine Corps's motto since 1883. (John Philip Sousa published the song in 1888.) These are solemn words to U.S. Marines. It is not uncommon for those who wear or have worn the uniform to carry this oath of honor throughout their lives, intensely loyal to their country, the Corps, and their fellow Marines. In wartime, many have sacrificed their lives to save those of others.

Since the establishment of the Corps in 1775, Marines have participated in 171 wars and expeditions, at a cost of more than 40,000 Marines' lives, with 189,000 wounded. Between 1862 and 1999, 301 Marines have been awarded the nation's highest military recognition, the Medal of Honor.

Except for the U.S. Coast Guard, the Marine Corps is the smallest of the U.S. military services. But it may, indeed, be the readiest, prepared at any time to fight on sea, on land, or in the air. As the thirty-first commandant of the Marine Corps, Gen. Charles Krulak, has put it, "The Marines really provide only two essential services to our nation. We make Marines; we win battles."

In this book, Anne Collier Rehill and I have endeavored to present accurately the stories of many who were, or still are, also actors. Ever prideful of their Marine experience, several of them told me that serving in the Corps had been the most real experience of their professional lives.

James E. Wise, Jr.

Acknowledgments

Col. Joseph H. Alexander, USMC (Ret.), read our work in search of historical errors, for which we are extremely grateful. Our deep thanks go to many others as well, including Natalie Hall for her essential part in making this book become a reality. Norman Hatch located many of the best photos, and David Murray Jaffe read the manuscript to ensure theatrical and cinematic accuracy. Among the many sources listed in the bibliography, *Leatherneck* magazine was especially helpful in providing military information.

Others who helped in various critical ways include Russell E. Arbus; Tom Baker; Barry Corbin; Edith Correale; Jerry Cross; Bradford Dillman; Dale Dye; Charles E. Ewing; Ann Ferrante; Robert W. Filkosky; Kirk Ford, Jr.; Lt. Col. John E. Forde, Jr., USMC (Ret.); M. Hill Goodspeed and the National Museum of Naval Aviation, Pensacola; Jack Green; Catherine Hayden; Bob Hunt; Col. Greg Johnson, USMC (Ret.); Kristine Krueger; Brigitte Kueppers; Cliff Lamb; Robert LaSalle; Janet Lorenz; the Marine Corps Historical Center, Washington, D.C.; Pamela Marvin; M. Sgt. Russell B. McGregor, USMC (Ret.); Nittany Leathernecks Detachment, Marine Corps League (Centre County, Penn.); Hugh O'Brian; Gerald O'Loughlin; Jean Ortiz; John R. Post; Jack Risler; Eddie Roberts; Col. John F. Shine, USMCR (Ret.); the U.S. Naval Institute; Col. William White, USMC (Ret.); E. C. "Buzz" Whitaker; Robert E. Wilson; and, as ever, our spouses, Carlotta and Brian.

PART 1

In the Heat of Battle

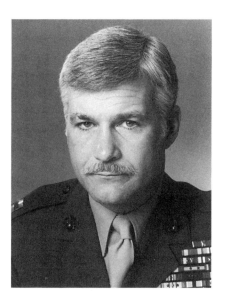

Dale Dye

Vietnam veteran and premier movie technical adviser Dale Adam Dye II got a humble start in life, in Cape Girardeau, Missouri, 8 October 1944. He was the only child of Della Grace (McCarty) Dye and World War II Navy veteran Dale Adam Dye, who served mostly in surface combatants in the South Pacific, on the deck force of combat auxiliaries. His father was one of the many who never found a way to fit in to everyday life after surviving a war in which he became part of a comradeship that was impossible to replace after the war was over. He told his son stories of his experiences with his band of brothers, and the younger Dale listened, captivated. He wanted to be part of that.

When the boy was thirteen years old, his father, who drowned too many sorrows in too much alcohol, killed himself. Della struggled on at her job in St. Louis, to provide her son with a decent education and a fighting chance at a good life. Dale, pleading to attend military school, completed his elementary years at St. Joseph's Military Academy in La Grange, Illinois. He then graduated as a cadet officer and battalion adjutant from Missouri Military Academy, Mexico, Missouri.

A rebel child who had not exactly made a habit of hitting the books, he had the ambition to attend the U.S. Naval Academy, but not the grades. Despite his thirst for more education, there was no money for college. Dye decided he should enlist in the Navy. He talked to recruiters, but found the service too vast. Dale wanted badly to distinguish himself somehow, and he needed a service that was not as populated as the Navy, one that tolerated nonconformists more than the other services, one in which he stood a reasonably good chance of reaching bayonet distance from the enemy.

In January 1964, Dye chose the Marine Corps, a decision with which he still derives tremendous satisfaction. The Corps shaped and molded him, he says; it sent him around the world, educated him, taught him to lead and to follow. Further, it introduced him to some of the most remarkable personalities in the history of this country.

Sent to Vietnam in 1965, he saw his first action around Chu Lai and Da Nang. He volunteered to return in 1967 and fought with Task Force X-Ray, 1st Marine Division, in the Phu Bai, Dong Ha tactical areas of operational responsibility (TAOR). While on patrols along the demilitarized zone and nearby areas, he became involved in frequent firefights and was twice wounded in action. The 1968 Tet Offensive found Dale Dye fighting in Hue City, where he was again wounded.

Dale Dye was honored with the Bronze Star for his heroic, selfless actions in Vietnam. "Frankly," he stated unassumingly in a 1998 letter to the authors, "the greatest honor involved for me was the fact that I was able to save a life or two (including my own) and discover that I had what it takes to face death and not flinch. That's a great, enduring gift that people who have not faced close-up enemy fire will never know."

His citation reads:

For heroic achievement in connection with operations against insurgent communist (Viet Cong) forces in the Republic of Vietnam while serving as a Combat Correspondent with the Informational Services

Office, 1st Marine Division. On 14 March 1968, during Operation Ford, Sergeant Dye was attached to Company E, Second Battalion, 3d Marines when an enemy explosive device was detonated, seriously wounding a Marine. Reacting instantly, he moved forward through the hazardous area and skillfully administered mouth-to-mouth resuscitation to the injured man. A short time later, the unit came under intense hostile fire which wounded two Marines. Disregarding his own safety, Sergeant Dye fearlessly ran across the fire-swept terrain and rendered first aid to the injured men while assisting them to covered positions. On 18 March 1968, Sergeant Dye again boldly exposed himself to intense enemy fire as he maneuvered forward to replace an assistant machine gunner who had been wounded. Undaunted by the hostile fire impacting around him, he skillfully assisted in delivering a heavy volume of effective fire upon the enemy emplacements. Although painfully wounded, he resolutely continued his determined efforts and was instrumental in silencing the fire from

At Headquarters Battalion, 1st Marine Division, DaNang, Vietnam, Battalion commander Lt. Col. O. K. Steele presents Dye with his second Purple Heart for wounds received in combat during Tet 1968 fighting in Hue City. (Dale Dye collection)

two hostile machine gun emplacements. Ignoring his painful injury, he steadfastly refused medical treatment, continuing to assist the machine gunner throughout the night. His heroic and timely actions were an inspiration to all who observed him and contributed significantly to the accomplishment of his unit's mission. Sergeant Dye's courage, sincere concern for the welfare of his comrades and steadfast devotion to duty in the face of great personal danger were in keeping with the highest traditions of the Marine Corps and of the United States Naval Service. Sergeant Dye is authorized to wear the Combat "V."

He returned briefly to the States in 1969 but soon volunteered to go back once again, finding the peacetime environment intolerable. This time he stayed in Vietnam until mid-1970, operating in the TAOR of Da Nang and points south. In all, he survived thirty-one major combat operations.

Unfortunately, while her son was recuperating in Japan from his last tour in Vietnam in 1970, Della Dye passed away, after suffering too much from a difficult life and, like her husband, drinking too much to ease the pain. Nevertheless, she apparently more than succeeded in her determination to provide Dale with a fighting chance at a decent life.

He went on to spend thirteen years as an enlisted man in the Corps, rising to the rank of master sergeant before being chosen for Officer Candidate School. He was appointed a chief warrant officer in 1976 and was later allowed to convert his commission to that of limited duty officer in the public-affairs field, appointed directly to first lieutenant.

While he served as public-affairs chief, he also qualified as a .45 pistol sharpshooter and expert and as an M-14 expert. He had reached the rank of captain by the time he was sent to Beirut with a multinational peacekeeping force. There, from 1982 to mid-1983, he served as assistant public-affairs officer for the 32d Marine Amphibious Unit, 24th MAU, and 22d MAU.

During his later years in the service, while carrying out assignments around the world in his capacity as public-affairs officer, Dye also earned his bachelor's degree in English from the University of Maryland. Upon his New Orleans retirement in 1984, aside from his Bronze Star with Combat "V," his decorations included three Purple Hearts,

Dye returned to Vietnam in 1969, here in A Shau Valley. As staff sergeant attached to 1st Marine Division, he accompanied a patrol from 1st Recon Battalion on a mission to observe enemy troop movements. (Dale Dye collection)

the Meritorious Service Medal (Okinawa), two Navy Commendation Medals with Combat "V" (Vietnam and Beirut), Navy Achievement Medal with Combat "V" (Vietnam), Joint Service Commendation Medal, Air Force Commendation Medal, Combat Action Ribbon (Vietnam and Beirut), Vietnamese Honor Medal First Class, and the Vietnamese Cross of Gallantry.

After leaving the service, Dye worked for a year at *Soldier of Fortune* magazine. He spent part of that time in Central America, reporting and training troops in guerrilla-warfare techniques in El Salvador and Nicaragua.

Next he moved on to Southern California, believing that he might be able to carve a niche for himself there, in an unusual and interesting way. He had tired of watching movies that frequently seemed to distort the realities of combat and the noble and generous spirit of a true warrior. Dye's mission was to change all that.

He began to ask around, meeting and greeting throughout Hollywood. Dale Dye discovered that he was at least as well qualified as many of those who were working in the field, with his twenty years in the Corps and having survived Vietnam. He not only had extensive firsthand knowledge about hand-to-hand combat and how to live in the jungle, he also was endowed with gusto and fearlessness in the social arena.

In his recon of Hollywood and the movie business, Dye had been surveying the trade publications regularly. In late 1985, he read that director Oliver Stone was going to make a film about Vietnam. But how to speak with him? Not through an agent, who would either give him the brush-off or want in on the deal. Dye stuck to what he knew: in a thought-out military strategy, he stepped up his socializing until he met someone who knew Stone and had his phone number. Then he simply called the director, told him he was a retired Marine who'd fought in Vietnam, and said that if Stone used his services, he would show it the way it really was.

The director, whose vision was to create authenticity through getting the details right, asked the aspiring consultant to come in for a meeting. He hired Dye to assist him in making the film *Platoon* (1986), in which Dye also appeared. It won the Academy Award for best picture of the year.

Since that smashing debut, the Vietnam vet has worked as technical adviser for many other directors as well, including Brian DePalma and Steven Spielberg. With more work than he could handle by himself, he formed the consulting group Warriors, Inc., with some of his other veteran comrades, to provide technical advice to the entertainment industry around the world. Their services include research, planning, staging, and on-set advising for directors and production people. They also train the actors.

That involves much more than showing actors how to hold a gun on the set. Actors are trained in one- to two-week, grueling schedules that incorporate elements of boot camp as well as infantry and special-operations schools. They are instructed in how to handle weapons, field-strip them, go on night patrols, and stand in formation.

Far from being treated like movie stars, they are forced to undergo training that approximates the real thing as closely as possible, including dealing with whatever real-life poisonous insects and reptiles may be out there in the California desert or the jungles of Thailand or the Philippines. And Dye not only wants the actors to get some idea of the realities of combat, he also wants to instill in them a profound respect for those who have died in the service of their country.

They emerge from their pseudo boot camp with a much clearer appreciation of the physical facts involved in surviving and fighting in often miserable conditions. They also develop an esprit de corps and friendships that have led some, including *Platoon*'s Tom Berenger and Willem Dafoe, as far as holding reunions.

The powerful, intense-eyed (blue), enthusiastic, handsome Dale Dye

Dale Dye *(second from left)* started his career as a technical adviser on *Platoon*. He confers here with *(from left)* Tom Berenger, Willem Dafoe, and Mark Moses. (Dale Dye collection)

has worked as both technical adviser and actor in several films, including *Casualties of War* (1989), *Always* (1989), *The Fourth War* (1990), and *Fire Birds* (1990). The many movies for which he has served as technical adviser include *Born on the Fourth of July* (1989), *Jacob's Ladder* (1990), *Last of the Mohicans* (1992), *Sniper* (1993), *Forrest Gump* (1994), *Outbreak* (1995), *Starship Troopers* (1997), and *Saving Private Ryan* (1998).

His television credits include appearing in and serving as technical adviser for the movies *Court-Martial of Jackie Robinson* (1990) and *Mission of the Shark* (1991) and the miniseries *Rough Riders* (1997); acting in the series *Supercarrier* (as the ship's commanding officer, Henry Madigan); and serving as technical adviser on the movies *Truman* (1995), *Vietnam War Story* (1988), and *By Dawn's Early Light* (1990).

For *Saving Private Ryan*, Dye *(standing, center)* worked on the beach at Wexford, Ireland, with Tom Hanks, Irish Army officers *(in berets)*, and Warriors, Inc., staffers *(front)*. (Dale Dye collection)

In 1997 the Marine Corps Combat Correspondents Association awarded Dale Dye the Brigadier General Robert L. Denig Award for outstanding contributions to the image of the Corps. That same year, he was honored with the Vietnam Veterans of America Excellence in Arts Award. Since leaving the Corps, he has also somehow found the time to publish five military novels.

An early marriage dissolved during the Vietnam War, and Dye later married a fellow Marine. They transferred around the world together for ten years before amicably divorcing, just before his retirement. He is now married to Kathryn Gwen Clayton, with whom he has produced one daughter. At their home in the San Fernando Valley, he fashions small animals for her out of wood and other natural elements. He also likes to shoot a rifle or pistol, does most of the smithing on his weapons, rides horses, and reads military history voraciously.

Sterling Hayden

"Something is wrong," wrote the troubled Sterling Hayden in his autobiography, *Wanderer* (Longmans, Green, 1964). The theme resonates uncomfortably throughout the work, permeating not only the author's periods of dejection but also his triumphs—in seafaring (his first and only lasting love, aside from his abiding bonds with his six children and his third wife, Catherine), acting, and the military. Hayden suffered from lifelong weltschmerz, always the seeker, at peace only when on the docks or out at sea.

He first shipped out at age sixteen, but he'd been ready to go for at least a year, since the day that he, his doting mother, and his stepfather landed in Boothbay Harbor, Maine. Out beyond the boats and the schooners, the sea sparkled endlessly, offering faraway horizons and ever-new possibilities. Drawn to the harbor as if by a glittering

(Catherine Hayden collection)

magnet, Sterling rented a rowboat for fifty cents the day after they arrived, and made his way out to three abandoned schooners. Clambering onboard, he lost himself in blissful, solitary exploration, imagining himself and his family living here.

Back in the rowboat, Sterling drifted to Tumbler Island, in the middle of the harbor, where he discovered a cottage for sale or rent. He managed to convince his parents that this tiny house, barely heated by a sheetmetal stove, was where they needed to spend the winter of 1931–32. The price was right, a deal was struck, and Sterling began one of the happiest years of his childhood.

With driftwood burning in the stove, the boy watched the sea day after day, sailing, in his mind, aboard the ships he saw coming in and out of the harbor. He visited the library every day, reading anything he could find about seafaring and ships; he befriended sailmakers and sailors. His transportation was a small boat that he sailed around the harbor, waving at ships' crews. Friendly, leathered sailors invited him aboard, where they regaled him with tales of afar. Sterling soaked it all in. Someday, he knew, these would be his exploits.

In the evenings after dinner—which his mother, Frances, managed to secure regularly, thanks to the kindness of the grocer—the young sailor bundled up and announced that it was time for him to go out on watch. He spent as long as he could on the island's dock, before Frances or Daddy Jim came out to bring him back inside.

But that was all right; he'd already envisioned the seafaring life that he would soon lead, if not the fine writing that he would eventually produce. Much later, after years of analysis and "false starts," Sterling Hayden published *Wanderer* (to be followed later by a novel, *Voyage,* Putnam, 1976), an eloquent and thoughtful look inward as well as a compelling account of a hair-raising life. It all began on 26 March 1916 in Upper Montclair, New Jersey.

George Woodruff and Frances Simonson Walter's only child, Sterling (born Montaigu, but his godfather convinced his parents that Sterling was preferable) Relyea Walter got a comfortable, if slightly dull, start in a safe, quiet, suburban neighborhood. Each and every two-week summer vacation was spent at Lake Minnewaska in the Catskills. George's work "in the ad game" ensured a satisfactory and steady income, which he maintained by taking the 7:18 train six mornings per week to New York, returning at 6:53 each evening. Frances kept house, tended to their son, and played her Steinway grand piano for hours at a time, to Sterling's delight.

Everything seemed headed for a predictable, if not exactly wild, future for the Walters. But then, after one of the many times Sterling misbehaved—this time involving a slingshot and a neighbor's wife driving by in a car—George took his son over his knee in the basement, administering a wet stick to his little behind. As Sterling screamed and George gave full vent to his anger, he suddenly collapsed and never fully recovered. Three months later he died, leaving his son to mourn him for a long time.

Now it was Frances's turn to commute to New York, to her new job at *Good Housekeeping* magazine. Her mother looked after Sterling and the house. Three years after her husband's death, Frances married James Watson Hayden, after he'd divorced his first wife. Hayden had some big deal in the air at the time, and they were all going to get rich and live a life of ease. Sterling was happy for his hardworking mother.

But the deal fell through, as it always would for "Daddy Jim." The family began a seemingly endless trek. Even though work was scarce at best, with the 1929 market crash, Frances always managed to make a few dollars by selling cosmetics door to door. But Daddy Jim remained jobless, hoping his next deal would succeed, and continuing to look as if it had, dressing in expensive suits and driving a Packard roadster.

As deal after deal failed to close over the years, Sterling tired of hearing the same old refrains. Many a dark night saw the Haydens sneaking away from a boarding house or a resort cottage, their bill unpaid. Sent to the Friends School in Washington, D.C. (and hating it, as he did all his schools, finally quitting for good after the tenth grade), Sterling had to leave, with the tuition bill unpaid. Finally Frances and James decided to try their luck up north, where they landed in Boothbay Harbor.

In 1932, at age sixteen, Sterling was enrolled at the Wassookeag School in Dexter, Maine, enjoying the experience about as much as he had all his other academic environments. His tales of seafaring interested no one other than a few schoolmates, and his behavior earned him repeated warnings that he'd best shape up. But Sterling preferred to ship out—besides, his stepfather was way behind in the tuition payments. Sterling decided to run away to Portland.

One November night after his roommates had fallen asleep, he slipped into the enormous, lighted closet, where he had everything waiting. He dressed silently in several layers of wool, snuck out the school's back entrance, and walked down the highway to a nearby diner. There he caught a ride with a truck driver into Bangor, elated at his new freedom, even in the chilly cab with its leaking windows, barreling through the icy night. Arriving in Bangor at the stroke of midnight, he ran to the train depot and hopped a train, following the procedure gleaned from his reading about the many hobos of those long years of the Great Depression.

He had a chance to verify some of that information, for when the train paused for a while, three real-life hobos materialized and made a small fire under a pail by the side of the tracks. They beckoned and he joined them, warming himself by their little hearth and learning that you always take a cigarette even if you don't want it—you can always use it to trade later.

In Portland he made his way to the fishing pier, where sailors let him spend one night on board a schooner, named, fittingly, the *Restless*. By morning he fancied himself a bona fide sailor too. But the real sailors told him to take his two dollars and get back home, finish school and learn a trade, then do his traveling after that. Having no idea what else to do, Sterling heeded their wisdom.

But soon the Haydens were on the move again. This time, with the Packard long gone, they took a bus to Boston and settled in a rooming house outside the city. Sterling walked five miles to Boston in search of an office job, Daddy Jim did not, and Frances sold cosmetics. The newspaper's help-wanted section was filled only with work-sought ads, and nobody had even a day's work to give the boy. Finally Sterling gave up on pounding the sidewalks of the business district and focused his search on the docks, where he wanted to be anyway. He spent a whole day on the wharves, asking crewman after crewman if he knew of an opening for an ordinary seaman. Only at the South Station fish pier did he stop asking: he had a pretty clear idea, by this time, of what it would be like to work in the frigid North Atlantic waters.

He hurried away, wondering if the whole idea was but a fantasy. On his shivering way home, he made his regular stop to gaze at the window display of a nautical-instruments shop. The shopkeeper called him in and told him about a big schooner, the *Puritan,* that was taking on men for an ocean journey from New London, Connecticut, to San Pedro, California. The captain had already agreed to sign on Hayden as ship's boy, at ten dollars a month.

Somewhat fond of his struggling stepfather in the beginning, by 1934 Sterling's feelings had changed. He secretly relished an epitaph he'd conjured up for Daddy Jim's gravestone: The Deal Is Closed. Sterling never would get to enjoy that gravestone, as Daddy Jim disappeared from their lives one day that year.

But now, with his previous *Puritan* experience, there was something Sterling could do to make a little money. He and Frances rode the train to Gloucester, a fishing town where hard times were a way of life. They would be at home there, they felt. Sure enough, strangers though they were, they were welcomed at the rooming house, and Sterling was welcomed at the docks by Capt. Ben Pine, who owned the Atlantic Supply Company and whose name was widely known in the seafaring world. He invited the lad in to warm himself by the stove, talked with him for a couple of hours, and then wrote a recommendation for him, addressed to the captains of fishing trawlers out of Boston. Leaving his sleeping mother a note, Sterling went immediately back to the train depot.

He worked aboard ships along the East Coast, by 1936 qualifying as first mate on board the schooner *Yankee,* his first round-the-world voyage. October 1938 found him working as mastheadsman on board Gloucester's *Gertrude L. Thebaud* in a three-out-of-five race against the *Bluenose,* from Nova Scotia. At the *Thebaud*'s helm was Capt. Ben Pine. By the third race, with the schooners tied, Pine hospitalized with an aggravated sinus condition, and the navigator out of commission too, Capt. Cecil Moulton took command of the *Thebaud* and a nervous Sterling Hayden became navigator.

The *Thebaud* won that race (but the *Bluenose* took the next two), and a Boston *Post* reporter singled out Hayden and Jack Hackett for their daring crawl along the spar in fierce winds: a block on the end of the main gaff had torn loose and had to be made secure. Not only that,

Hayden cut quite a dashing figure, with his Viking good looks—over six feet tall, sun-bleached hair, strong. The *Post* compared him to a "movie idol" and New England reporters began to take notice as the "Viking" brought ships in and out of ports. He and fellow sailor (and artist) Lawrence O'Toole befriended one newspaperman who haunted the docks almost as much as they did—Associated Press reporter Tom Horgan.

Considered a natural-born sailor, in November Hayden was given command of his first ship. He was twenty-two years old, hired to sail the Ceylon brigantine *Florence C. Robinson* from Gloucester to Tahiti. The newspapers hailed the little ship's departure and her February arrival in Tahiti, manned by a hearty crew of eleven, including O'Toole. They had braved furious storms to get there, and they reveled for six months in Paradise. Hayden fell in love for the first time and became engaged to marry a nineteen-year-old beauty named Mano (he later called off the wedding, believing that he could not make her happy). But first he would buy his own ship, the steel schooner *Aldebaran,* and start a packet service, running between Honolulu and Tahiti.

To complete the purchase of the *Aldebaran,* the former kaiser's yacht, which was laid up in Panama, Hayden had to sail her to Boston and get her inspected. But a violent storm off Cape Hatteras swamped the vessel, which had to be towed to Charleston after the Coast Guard rescued the crew. Now Hayden was broke.

It was the end of 1939; in Europe, the German military machine was on the march. In Massachusetts, Tom Horgan and Larry O'Toole convinced Sterling Hayden to try Hollywood. Horgan promptly wrote to an agent he knew, and O'Toole accompanied him to New York, where he knew another agent. In the end, Hayden signed with Paramount Studios at six hundred dollars a month, and he and Frances moved to Hollywood.

The studio, like many others at the time, groomed lookers such as the Viking for stardom. They gave him acting lessons and sent him to the gym; he got the full treatment, and he hated it all. He was sent on publicity tours, which he found ridiculous. He even went to the White House, where Franklin Delano and Eleanor Roosevelt hosted an event for thespians—including Lana Turner, Greer Garson, Gene Kelly, and Danny Kaye—who'd contributed their efforts to the 1941 March of

Dimes. As they said good-bye, Hayden told the president that Capt. Ben Pine sent greetings, and was surprised to learn that FDR knew all about the 1938 *Thebaud* and *Bluenose* race.

His first movie was *Virginia* (1941), in which he played opposite his future first wife, Madeleine Carroll, and Fred MacMurray. Smitten with Carroll from the start, Hayden struggled to develop his new acting skills through the summer of 1940. That same year he appeared in *Bahama Passage* (1941), again opposite Carroll, liking the movie industry less all the time.

Hayden wanted to do something real, something that mattered, something for which he could respect himself as a man. Seafaring was hard, but real—and so was the war. Carroll talked all the time about getting involved in it. Finally, after honestly explaining his feelings as best he could, Sterling Hayden left Paramount on good terms.

In late November 1941, he contacted Col. William "Wild Bill" Donovan, Coordinator of Information. COI, an intelligence-collecting and covert-operations agency established by the president, later became the Office of Strategic Services, or OSS, forerunner of the Central Intelligence Agency. Donovan arranged for Hayden to receive commando and parachute training in Glasgow.

After a miserable convoy crossing, he reported to a London office where no one had expected him or seemed to care that he was there. Nevertheless, after a few days they got him processed and off to Glasgow, where he trained. In March 1942 he jumped out of a Stirling bomber and 'chuted into a quarry, where he broke his ankle, tore up his knee, and knocked his backbone around.

They fixed him up and sent him back to the States, where he married Madeleine Carroll in a lodge in New Hampshire, by a fireplace. Like her husband, Carroll was cynical at best about Hollywood and the film industry. She gave up her movie career, joined the American Red Cross, and was sent to Europe.

Hayden wanted to join the Navy and requested a lieutenant's commission and command of a PT boat. Because he lacked even a high-school diploma, the Navy countered with an ensign's ranking and no guarantee of a PT boat assignment. So on 26 October 1942, Sterling Hayden enlisted in the Marine Corps and was sent to Parris Island, South Carolina, for boot training.

This was not an easy experience for a movie star, even a reluctant

After boot training at Parris Island and being retained as a drill instructor, Hayden went to OCS and changed his name to John Hamilton.

one; it was especially rough for an independent, individualistic, freedom lover who felt at home only on the open seas. But he toughed it out, learned the ropes, and turned out to be a "hell of a good Marine," according to his drill instructor, Pvt. George S. Featherstone, who added, "Life as a DI would be a pleasure if all were as good recruits" (U.S. Marine Corps Division of Public Relations release, 2 December 1942). One of two in his platoon selected for Office Candidate School after boot training, Hayden spent three weeks as a drill instructor before he left.

Reporting to the Marine Corps Schools Command at Quantico,

Virginia, he was assigned to the Twenty-Third Officer Candidates Class. Upon his completion, he was commissioned second lieutenant, USMCR, on 21 April 1943. Hayden was a good Marine on the surface. But he loathed the discipline and the fact that he was so easily recognized, which worked against him in the Corps. Carroll and he no longer wanted to be associated with Hollywood; Hayden wanted to be thought of as just another Marine. They went to court to have their last name changed to Hamilton. Sterling changed his first name too, and by late June 1943 he was legally John Hamilton.

Even so, he felt the by-now familiar urge to get out of the situation he was in—only this time he was wearing a uniform. He'd been working on the problem since before commissioning, though, and had again reached Colonel Donovan, in charge of the OSS in Washington. John Hamilton asked to be considered for the secret service. Accordingly, when his class members received their orders, most were sent to the Pacific, but Hayden and two others went to the OSS.

Reporting to Temporary Building Q near the Lincoln Memorial, where the OSS was headquartered, Hayden found himself surrounded by a hodgepodge of businessmen, enlisted men, and junior officers from all the services. It was the summer of 1943, and the agency was just getting its confused start. Assignments and plans were developed in secrecy from everybody else, but they all had one goal in common— to torment the enemy in every way possible. Eventually, Hayden was ordered to Cairo.

He was greeted by a colonel who had no idea that his unit was about to add a new agent, nor what he was supposed to do with him. After several months the colonel ordered him to Bari, Italy, to lend support to the head of the Yugoslav partisan fighters, Marshal Tito. Tito led a Communist band that was proving to be quite successful in sabotaging German efforts in their occupied country. Hayden's assignment was to set up a partisan base of operations at the port city of Monopoli, south of Bari.

He took command of some four hundred Yugoslav partisans—fifty of them female—and fourteen schooners, six ketches, and two brigantines. Their mission: to transport supplies across the Adriatic Sea to Tito's guerrillas. After running the German blockade out of Italy, they unloaded the supplies, hastily and under cover of darkness, on Vis, a

Second Lt. John Hamilton *(right)* was assigned to the OSS and sent to Monopoli, Italy, from where he transported supplies across the Adriatic to Tito's guerrillas.

partisan-held island off Dalmatia. Fishing boats then made their treacherous way to the mainland, unloading between Nazi-held beaches. From there, burro trains transported the supplies up into the mountains, to the partisans.

Hayden was entranced by these fierce Yugoslav partisans. He had been intrigued by communism before, having heard noises about it in Hollywood and along the waterfront in Oakland. Now, watching these partisan guerrillas, fighters who were tougher and more dedicated than anyone he'd ever known, he felt inspired and wrote long letters to his friends back home about them. It was this experience that played an important role in his later decision to join the American Communist Party.

In 1944, Hayden and two others parachuted behind enemy lines in Yugoslavia and led several downed Allied aviators to safety in Italy.

A much-respected commanding officer, Hayden was awarded the Silver Star for his service during the Balkan tour. His citation reads:

> John Hamilton 022085, Captain [as of February 1945], United States Marine Corps Reserve, for gallantry in action in the Mediterranean Theater of Operations from 24 December 1943 to 2 January 1944. Captain Hamilton displayed great courage in making hazardous sea voyages in enemy infested waters, and reconnaissances through enemy held areas. His conduct reflected great credit upon himself and the United States Armed Forces.

His other decorations included the World War II Victory Medal; the European-African-Middle Eastern Campaign Medal with two bronze stars and a bronze arrowhead (bronze star for participation in the Naples-Foggia campaign, bronze star for action against the enemy in the Balkan countries, bronze arrowhead for parachuting into enemy-held territory); a Letter of Commendation; and the Yugoslav Government Order of Merit. These awards were given by the OSS, shrouded, at the time, in secrecy.

After completing his duties in the Balkans and enjoying thirty days' leave in the States—Carroll stayed at her post in Italy—Hayden flew back to Europe to join an OSS group in Germany. But in Paris he was ordered instead to the First Army in Belgium, which had just fought the Battle of the Bulge. There, assisted by six technical sergeants who were fluent in German, he followed the troops' advance from Cologne to Marburg in a mostly fruitless search for authentic anti-Nazis. He spent the summer of 1945 making bomb-damage assessments of ports in Germany, Norway, and Denmark.

In September he visited Carroll in Paris, where she had been transferred, and where the Hamiltons mutually and amicably, if somewhat uncomfortably, agreed that they no longer had a relationship. They were divorced in Reno later that year, Hayden handling the paperwork by himself. He was discharged from active duty on 24 December 1945 and remained in the reserves until 1948.

Hayden returned to Hollywood, where he was warmly welcomed and signed with Paramount, which did not keep him from turning in an excellent lead performance for MGM in John Huston's *The Asphalt*

Jungle (1950). He had ideas about helping to change the world, fighting fascism. Still fascinated by the exploits of his partisan friends from the war, and believing that Marxism offered a better life for more than just the privileged few, he drifted into the communist crowd in the film industry and joined the Party. He attended meetings but was soon disillusioned with the dogmatic, all-knowing atmosphere. Six months after joining, he canceled his membership. It would come back to haunt him, in the form of the ignominious House Un-American Activities Committee.

In April 1951, Hayden fully cooperated with the HUAC, including naming names. He immediately—and permanently—regretted doing so, and joined the effort to abolish the HUAC. After that brief and humiliating hiatus, Hayden went on to make many more films, including *Johnny Guitar* (1954), *The Last Command* (1955), *The Killing* (1956), *Dr. Strangelove: Or How I Learned to Stop Worrying and Love the Bomb* (1964, in which he brilliantly played the mad Gen. Jack D. Ripper, whose chief concern was to safeguard his precious bodily fluids), *The Godfather* (1972; his brief performance as a dirty cop was, again, outstanding), *The Long Goodbye* (1973, earning more plaudits), and *9 to 5* (1980). He also appeared on live TV in the fifties and sixties, including *Playhouse 90* and a DuPont Show of the Month, and he gave fine performances in several made-for-TV movies.

Despite the successes, Sterling Hayden was not talented at managing his finances. Until after his last trip to Tahiti at age forty-three, he did not believe in having money that one had not earned, and he spent nearly everything that he earned. He abhorred the shallowness and glitz of Hollywood; he had mixed feelings, at best, about his acting profession. His second marriage had come to a rocky conclusion—in May 1947, he had married Betty Ann De Noon, a union that lasted for eight years and produced four children. He felt like he had to do something to feel like a man rather than a robot.

So in 1959 he went back to sea, sailing his schooner, the *Wanderer*, to Tahiti. In defiance of a court order not to leave Los Angeles with the four kids (he had won custody), Hayden scared up the needed cash and sailed with all four of them, and a crew of eleven who worked for no pay. They did it purely for an adventure that inspired people all over the world to write to Hayden, cheering him on.

They sailed on 20 January, and after a sometimes very hairy voyage, made it to Tahiti on 4 March. They spent nearly a year there, during which Hayden began to write, while his children were tutored by one of the crew. But after a while life became routine again, and they may as well have been in California, where the children could go to a real school. It was time to go home. He hustled up the cash and sailed. A year after leaving L.A., the court sentenced him to a five-hundred-dollar fine and five days in jail for contempt of court—and a suspended sentence.

Sterling Hayden married Catherine Denise McConnell in 1960 and added two more offspring to his brood. When he died in 1986, at the age of seventy, Catherine, the children, and close friends scattered his ashes off Point Sausalito, over the San Francisco Bay.

Parris Island

The site of one of the first European colonies in the New World, Parris Island pro-
vides basic training to all Marines east of the Mississippi. The Spanish landed
here in 1526, followed by the French Huguenots in 1592 and then the Barbadans
in 1663. In 1670 the English landed last and dug in, starting plantations across
the approximately 7,800 acres of land and water off the South Carolina coast,
midway between Charleston and Savannah.

The South Carolina Lord Proprietors passed down the area's land title through
various colonial settlers, until 1715. At that point, Alexander Parris, who had long
served as South Carolina's public treasurer, acquired the island, leaving it with his
name.

During the Civil War, in 1861, a group of seamen and U.S. Marines captured
the island and two nearby forts, Beauregard and Walker. But the first official
Marine Corps activity did not take place here until thirty years later. On 26 June
1891, a small Marine detachment reported for duty in connection with the U.S.
Naval Station, Port Royal, South Carolina, on Parris Island. Two years later in
1893, this detachment received the highest commendation for its work during
a hurricane and tidal wave.

A school for officers was established on Parris Island in 1909, and in 1911,
the first drill instructors arrived with two recruit companies. But they were transferred to Charleston and Norfolk that same year, and the Navy took over the barracks. When Parris Island was returned to the Corps in 1915, the drill instructors came back and reestablished recruit training there. Since that time, Parris
Island has been a major Marine training base.

During World War I, 41,000 Marine recruits were trained here. In August
1940, recruit training was organized along battalion lines, and when the country
entered World War II, the island was flooded with both recruits and the personnel to train them. With the enlarging of the base, almost 205,000 recruits were
trained at Parris between 1941 and 1945. When the Japanese surrendered,
more than 20,000 new Marines were training here.

Rapid demobilization at the end of World War II depopulated the island to
the point that, just before Korea, only two recruit battalions were training and the
total population barely reached 2,350. But in March 1952, that number jumped
to 24,424, as recruits were trained, and during the course of the war in Korea,
more than 138,000 Marines were trained at Parris Island.

In 1958 the barracks were redesignated Recruit Training Regiment, controlling all activities pertaining to the training of recruits. Through the years, Parris
Island has remained the boot camp for those who join the Corps in the eastern
half of the United States. (The Marine Corps Recruit Depot at San Diego serves
the western half of the nation.) Presently, some 15,000 men and women annu-
ally receive their basic training at this historic facility.

Louis Hayward

An actor since age six, when he imitated Charlie Chaplin for his mother's entertainment, Louis Hayward went on performing for the rest of his life, charming leading ladies and audiences on both sides of the Atlantic with his debonair manner. He was born with the name Seafield Grant (and was later also known as Charles Louis Hayward) in Johannesburg, South Africa. Shortly before his 19 March 1909 birth, his father, a mining engineer, met with an untimely demise in an accident. His mother, Agatha, soon relocated to London, raising and educating her son there and in Brittany, France.

With an early taste for acting, the young Hayward was given lessons and training. Eventually he joined a company that toured England's provinces, and later he settled in London, where he managed a night-club. One evening playwright Noel Coward came to the club, and, after a chat with Hayward, offered him a bit part in a production of F. P. Huntley's *Dracula*. It was an excellent entree to the big time. Hayward's first appearance in a film followed—*Self-Made Lady* (1932)—as well as several more plays and films before he crossed the ocean to the New World.

There, after meeting famous Broadway actor Alfred Lunt, he was cast in the Broadway play *Point Valaine,* winning 1934's New York Critics Award for his highly acclaimed performance. He then appeared in a few unexceptional movies before playing Denis Moore in *Anthony Adverse* (1936), after which Louis Hayward began to be considered a star. Major roles followed in swashbucklers such as *The Man in the Iron Mask* (1939), in which he played Louis XIV and Philippe, and *The Son of Monte Cristo* (1940).

Hollywood also introduced him to his dazzling first wife, actress Ida Lupino, whom he married in 1938. Their mountainside home, overlooking the Santa Monica Bay, became a favorite gathering spot for fireside visits and candlelit dinners with other actors, artists, and friends. Hayward became a naturalized American citizen on 6 December 1941, the day before the Japanese attack on Pearl Harbor.

On 8 June 1942, he quietly enlisted in the U.S. Marine Corps. With his substantial background in the film industry and his technical knowledge of how to compose and produce an effective image on film, he was commissioned on 1 July 1942 as a first lieutenant, appointed for aviation photographic duty.

In July 1942, he joined the Marine Schools Detachment at Quantico, Virginia, appointed as director, Marine Corps Photographic Section. He remained in this position, making training films for the Corps, until January 1943, when he was ordered to the 2d Marine Division, Fleet Marine Force, in the field. He was promoted to the temporary rank of captain on 2 February 1943.

On 28 March, Hayward joined the 2d Marine Division's Headquarters Company, Division Headquarters Battalion, Division Special Troops, in the Pacific, as assistant D-2 photographic officer. One of his assignments was to drive all around New Zealand with a camera crew in two vehicles, making a documentary about the recovery of wounded, malaria-ridden, and battle-fatigued Marines who had fought at Guadalcanal and nearby islands. The men had been sent to

Marines move out from the beachhead on Tarawa, November 1943.

live on farms, where they helped shear the sheep and do the planting and whatever other chores they were capable of. It was believed that working in the fields in this healthy, stable environment speeded recovery time and rebuilt strength far more effectively than the same time spent in a hospital, a theory that Louis Hayward and his crew helped to substantiate.

In October 1943, Hayward and part of his photo staff embarked aboard the USS *Zeilin* at Wellington, New Zealand, and sailed north to participate in landing maneuvers at Efate Island in the New Hebrides. Then it was on to the Gilbert Islands, where they went ashore with the Marines at Betio in the Tarawa atoll on 20 November 1943. Many of Hayward's photographers had already been at Guadalcanal, but not even that butchery had prepared them for this.

The atoll was heavily defended by highly trained Japanese sailors and proved to be one of the most costly island invasions in the history of the Corps. Landing craft stalled on reefs because of low tide waters, which meant the Marines had to wade five hundred yards to reach the beaches. But as they moved through the water, they were cut down by Japanese snipers. Meanwhile, stationary and incoming landing craft were repeatedly destroyed by shore batteries.

Hayward's photographic team captured everything on film: preparations for transport, the battle (they were on the front lines and armed), the horrible aftermath, and the landing of the first plane on the now U.S.-held airstrip. Split up between 2d Marine Division assault units in landing craft, the photographers made it ashore with one wounded and some equipment lost in the water. Their mission was to obtain photographs and 16mm footage for study in future operations.

They stayed with the Leathernecks throughout the seventy-six hours it took to wrest Tarawa from the control of its resolute Japanese defenders. Shooting both film and guns, at the end of the battle Hayward's team had about nine hundred photos and five thousand feet of movies in Photochron (early color film).

As Hayward jumped from his landing craft, shots were ringing all around him and fighting men dropped. The Marines who made it to the beach that first day clung to a narrow strip of sand as the Japanese poured heavy fire at them. Had the Japanese known how weak the Marine force was, they might have pushed their enemy back into the sea. But heavy bombardment from American warships offshore had severed the Japanese aboveground communications lines, and their units had become isolated. The Japanese fought on, with no idea how effective they had been in crippling the initial assault.

More landings were made during the early morning hours of the second day, and by sheer courage and tenacious fighting, the Marines pushed inland off the beaches. Hayward and crew snapped away, trying to stay alive while photographing the hell into which they had been dropped. The island fell after more than seventy hours, in a battle that killed more than a thousand Americans and four thousand of their enemies.

Their photo coverage of the battle was sent back to Washington for processing and viewing by the Joint Staff, and director Frank Capra was asked to study the footage. The result was the historic film *With the Marines at Tarawa,* which won the Academy Award for best documentary of 1944.

A weighted-down Marine gets a moment for a smoke with a buddy during the battle of Tarawa.

Following the battle, on 3 December 1943, Hayward sailed for Honolulu on board the USS *President Monroe*. From there he was flown to California, where he joined Ida. He came home a changed man: pale, withdrawn, deeply disturbed about the violent death he had managed to crawl away from while leaving so many others there forever. From time to time he began to tell Ida some things about Tarawa, but then he would fall suddenly silent.

Hayward was assigned temporary duty in Hollywood for the purpose of processing "certain films." He was then assigned to assist in processing the film footage for the final cut of *With the Marines at Tarawa*. Day after day he had to relive the battle, shown in grotesque scenes that the general public would never see. He grew even more moody and nervous at home and suffered severe asthma attacks. In the end, he and Ida, unable to recover their former intimacy, separated, remaining on friendly and mutually supportive terms.

After the battle, most of those who had snapped photos and filmed footage throughout remained physically, if not emotionally, unscathed. Their film earned the Academy Award for best documentary of 1944. Hayward is in back row, second from left.

In June 1944, while still attached to Headquarters Company, Hayward was detached to the Marine Barracks, Naval Operating Base, Terminal Island, San Pedro, California. Suffering from severe depression followed by a complete physical collapse, he spent his remaining two months in the Corps as a patient at the Corona and Long Beach naval hospitals.

When Hayward was released from active duty on 7 August 1944, his temporary captain's commission automatically reverted to his former rank of first lieutenant. He was awarded the Bronze Star with Combat "V," with the following citation:

For meritorious service as Assistant Intelligence Officer in Charge of Combat Photography of the Second Marine Division, prior to and during operations against Japanese forces on Tarawa, Gilbert Islands, from 20 to 28 November 1943. Personally going ashore with the assault units of the division despite grave hazards, Captain Hayward skillfully and daringly directed his men in their efforts throughout the battle and afterwards while photographing enemy defenses for intelligence studies. By his efficient preparation in training his men in all phases and techniques of combat photography and his tireless leadership ashore, he succeeded in producing a comprehensive and technically excellent coverage of our forces in battle. Captain Hayward's professional ability, courageous conduct and tireless devotion to duty were in keeping with the highest traditions of the United States Naval Service. Captain Hayward is authorized to wear the Combat "V."

He was honorably discharged from the Corps on 9 November 1944, entitled as well to wear the American Area Campaign Medal, the Asiatic-Pacific Area Campaign Medal, and the World War II Victory Medal. His crew members wore similar campaign medals and were awarded Navy Commendation ribbons.

Louis Hayward eventually recovered from his breakdown and went on to make many more films, including *And Then There Were None* (1945), *The Return of Monte Cristo* (1946), *Fortunes of Captain Blood* (1950), *The Son of Dr. Jekyll* (1951), and *Terror in the Wax Museum* (1973). He made about twenty movies in all, becoming one of the first actors to successfully negotiate a percentage from the profits of his on-film work. His television series included *The Lone Wolf* (1954–55), *The Pursuers* (1963), and *Survivors* (1969–70).

He was married twice more after his 1945 divorce from Lupino: to socialite Margaret Morrow Field and then to model June Blanchard, the mother of his son. He smoked three packs a day for more than fifty years, attributing to the habit the lung cancer that killed him in 1985, at the age of seventy-five.

Brian Keith

R obert Brian Keith, Jr., was born (14 November 1921) on the
road. His parents, actors Robert and Helena Shipman Keith,
were touring with a theater company when the time came for
Helena to make a stop in Bayonne, New Jersey. She recuperated there
with Junior for a month, then rejoined the rest of the company in Rich-
mond, Virginia.

The Keiths moved around for the next seven years to wherever they
could find work on the stage. When "talkies" came along, Robert
Senior went to Hollywood, where he was featured in about thirty
movies and wrote screenplays. Helena preferred a more normal com-
munity environment for Junior, so she moved to Long Island and
opened a gift shop.

Brian's first and only childhood film appearance came at age three

(Photofest)

in *The Pied Piper of Malone* (1924). At age eight, he sold newspapers and *Liberty* magazines for ten cents apiece. He also read the magazine, devouring "War Dog" column stories of Marines in China, at Belleau Wood, wherever their exploits took them. He devoured other information about them, too, including books by Marines such as John William Thomason, author of *Fix Bayonets* (1926).

Captivated by all this Marine Corps lore, Brian Keith had made up his mind before his country got into World War II. In the summer of 1941 he enlisted in the Marine Corps Reserve, finding work at the Grumman Aircraft factory on Long Island.

Shortly after Pearl Harbor he was ordered to Parris Island for boot camp, where he rated expert on the rifle and pistol ranges. That resulted in his next assignment: marksmanship instructor at the Officers Candidate School, Quantico.

In the summer of 1942, the Marines landed at Guadalcanal, in the Solomon Islands. The United States was finally going on the offensive against the Japanese in the Pacific. Keith was ordered to San Diego, then transported by ship to Hawaii, then to Midway, back to Hawaii, and finally to Bougainville. There he was assigned to VMSB-244, as a rear gunner in SBD Douglas Dauntless dive bombers.

These bombers were used on missions against the major Japanese base at Rabaul, located to the northwest on the island of New Britain. The flight path to Rabaul from Henderson Field, Guadalcanal, was like a shooting gallery, known as the Valley of Death because of the number of lives it claimed from both the skies and the seas.

Japanese fighters rose to meet their enemy from small fields on islands along the way; more Japanese planes launched from Rabaul. In the ruthless air battles that resulted, many planes fell to the seas riddled by machine-gun fire, some burning and exploding on the way down. Meanwhile, at the same time that Marines were fighting for Guadalcanal, enemy ships were trying to reinforce the island by landing troops under cover of night.

Dive-bombing was not an independently executed operation: it involved a coordinated effort between three separate layers of air cover. The top layer, at twenty thousand to thirty thousand feet, was covered by Army Air Corps P-38 Lockheed Lightnings and P-51 Mustangs. Next, at fifteen thousand feet, came Marine F4U Corsairs—

often the renowned Black Sheep squadron commanded by Maj. Gregory "Pappy" Boyington, USMCR. New Zealanders flying P-40 Kittyhawks provided the lowest-altitude cover at ten thousand feet and below. The Army Air Corps called these aircraft, which the Flying Tigers had used earlier in China, Curtiss Warhawks.

The Flying Tigers, with shark's teeth painted on their forward fuselages, consisted of about ninety U.S. pilots who had been retired or discharged from the Army Air Corps, Navy, and Marine Corps. They were designated the American Volunteer Group (AVG), and they flew outdated Curtiss P-40 fighters from airfields in China, led by retired Maj. Gen. Claire Chennault. Between 20 December 1941 and 4 July 1942, these acclaimed "soldier-of-fortune" aviators were responsible for downing nearly three hundred Japanese aircraft. After their country officially entered World War II, they were redesignated the U.S. China Air Task Force.

Joining the operational fleet in December 1941, for the next two years the SBD Dauntless became the workhorse for carrier aerial dive-bombing. Though slow and vulnerable, the plane was rugged and could withstand destructive fire from enemy aircraft. The Dauntless was slated to be replaced by the Curtiss SB2C Helldiver, but it remained in the fleet long after it was supposed to be gone. It was a main factor in the United States's victory at Midway, the turning point in the war against Japan.

The SBD Dauntless carried a crew of two: the pilot and the rear gunner. In addition to bombs, the pilot could fire .50-caliber machine guns from wing ports, while the rear gunner was tasked with keeping the enemy off the aircraft's tail as it made its dive-bombing attacks. The gunner had little firepower with twin .30-caliber machine guns; nevertheless, the guns were effective for their job of keeping Japanese Zeroes at a distance.

Keith survived quite a few hair-raising rides, dive-bombing at ninety-degree angles while firing out the back of the plane, taking hits at the same time from ground antiaircraft guns. He never was wounded and never had to bail out, even though his aircraft got a three-foot-long hole in one of the wings and his earphones got shot off. In a November 1992 interview with *Marines* magazine, he talked about a close call, one of many times when two Zeroes were on their tail. "My gun overheated from firing and they were still coming," he said. "In desperation, I shot double red flares at them. Help arrived just in time when a Navy pilot shot one of them down. Unfortunately, the other Zero shot him down."

Nor was there was much rest for the weary after air combat. Back on Bougainville, where Japanese guerrillas were still active around their airfield, incoming mortar and machine-gun fire were far from rare events. Keith and his buddies might be playing cards or relaxing outside when they suddenly had to hit the dirt: the tireless Japanese had again penetrated inside the perimeter. Sometimes they simply charged at the Americans, whether or not they were sufficiently armed to carry out their fanatic attack.

Keith flew missions for two years against Rabaul and the nearby Japanese-held islands. The Allied strategy was to bypass Rabaul in their Southwest Pacific island-hopping toward the Japanese mainland. By relentless bombing, they effectively kept the base out of commission, so that Japan never had an opportunity to mount a rear offensive from that area.

Sgt. Brian Keith finally returned to the States in December 1944. After enjoying thirty days of Christmas leave at home on Long Island, he was sent to Oak Grove, North Carolina. His assignment there was to fly as rear gunner for pilots training in a new high-powered aircraft, the SB2C Curtiss-Wright Helldiver. This was a terrifying experience, resulting in a permanent back injury for another trainer with whom Keith was friends. Keith would have preferred to take his chances against the Japanese at Leyte Gulf, but that was not to be.

One final violent event marked his exit from the service: while celebrating V-J Day in a bar in Miami, Keith got caught up in a brawl and wound up having to choose between ninety days in the brig and getting busted down to corporal. So, after managing to emerge in one piece from the Pacific War and then training duty in Helldivers, Cpl. Brian Keith was honorably discharged from the Marine Corps in 1945.

A future as a professional actor, following in the family tradition, was more appealing now, and the husky, golden-haired Keith began to work in stock theater. From there he moved to radio, and then to television, where he appeared on programs including *The Lux Video Theater, Motorola TV Hour, Pepsi Cola Playhouse,* and *Studio One.* He

A squadron of Dauntless dive bombers, Guadalcanal, 1943.

starred in the *Crusader* series (1955–56) and made it onto Broadway in *Mr. Roberts*, followed by *The Moon Is Blue* and *Darkness of Noon*.

Offered a contract by Paramount Studios in 1951, Brian Keith appeared in *Arrowhead* (1953, opposite Charlton Heston and Jack Palance). More than fifty movies followed, in which he earned lasting respect as a talented and versatile, professionally minded actor. His portrayals include those in *The Young Philadelphians* (1959); *Ten Who Dared* (1960); *Nevada Smith* (1966); *The Russians Are Coming, The Russians Are Coming* (1966); *Reflections in a Golden Eye* (1967); *Krakatoa, East of Java* (1969); *Suppose They Gave a War and Nobody Came* (1970); *The Wind and the Lion* (1975, in which Keith played Teddy Roosevelt); *Moonraker* (1979); and *Death Before Dishonor* (1986).

Keith was featured in many television series in addition to *Crusader,* including *The Westerner, Family Affair, The Brian Keith Show, Archer, Hardcastle and McCormick, Pursuit of Happiness, Walter and Emily,* and *Major Dad* (in 1992).

After an episode of the *Major Dad* show filmed before a live audience, actor Gerald McRaney (the character Maj. J. D. "Mac" MacGillis) presented Keith with a plaque of the Marine Corps emblem and K-bar, on behalf of the cast. "We play Marines," he said, "you're the real thing. It was our privilege to work with you." To go with the plaque, Shanna Reed (reporter Polly Cooper on the show) gave him a set of silver-plated *Major Dad* dog tags.

In 1988—better late than never—at Marine Corps Air Station El Toro, California, Keith was presented with an Air Medal for services in the Solomon Islands from 18 October to 4 December 1943, the Asiatic-Pacific Campaign Medal with three bronze stars, the World War II Victory Medal, and rifle and pistol badges. As with so many others who served in World War II, sometimes such awards were lost in the mountains of postwar paperwork and were never presented to their recipients. Keith's awards came as a result of a letter to the commandant of the Marine Corps, Gen. P. X. Kelley, from a Marine who had served with Keith during the Solomons campaign. Upon checking the wartime records, the Corps verified that the actor was, indeed, eligible to receive these awards.

During his visit to El Toro, Keith looked over a restored TBM Avenger, and periodically he had to stop himself from jumping up and booming out "Yes, sir!" But his most vivid Corps memory, he told reporters, was boot camp. His drill instructors' names were forever etched in his mind.

Married twice—to Judy Landon and then Victoria Young—Brian Keith delighted in his own real-life family of six children. He died in 1997.

Lee Marvin

More than rough around the edges, Lee Marvin was a true wild one from the time he was a boy. Kicked out of nearly every despised school he attended, Marvin was not just physical, he could be downright violent. He both worked and played hard, imbibing gargantuan quantities of beer, whiskey, vodka, tequila—whatever was available. During parties at his house on the beach at Malibu, which could spring up spontaneously at any time of the night or day, he might line up the glasses on the bar and start a shooting contest.

His gun collection was his most prized possession, and he slept with a sharpened axe within reach. The local police were all too familiar with Lee Marvin's stunts, such as driving on some imagined vital errand to the airport in the middle of the night clothed in a bathrobe and hairnet. Nor were his bar brawls infrequent events.

(Pam Marvin collection)

But he was also understanding, kind, and steadfast, remaining on good terms with his first wife after their strife-free divorce and maintaining close ties with his four children. After his discharge from the Marines, he missed the esprit de corps so much that he tried twice to reenlist and attended 4th Marine Division reunions frequently. In the movie industry, he worked hard to make his fellow performers look their best. Lee Marvin was a team player.

This quality, as well as his machismo, had been passed down from his forebears. Among them were the first chief justice of Connecticut, a Union general, and a professor who went on Polar expeditions with Adm. Robert E. Peary. His father, Lamont, who himself boasted an extensive collection of guns, enlisted as a soldier in the First World War and went to France with the American Expeditionary Forces. Surviving, he was made a captain and was decorated. Lamont trained his sons, early on, how to handle a gun, so that by the time Lee hit boot camp, what was new to the other enlistees was just playtime for the war hero's son.

The boys' mother, Courtenay D. Marvin, wrote for Helena Rubinstein and magazines such as *Photoplay* in New York City, specializing in fashion and beauty. Lamont worked as an advertising executive and was in charge of the New York and New England Apple Institute. The Marvins had two sons, Robert (who became an artist and teacher) and Lee (19 February 1924), raising them in the city until 1940, when Lamont became advertising manager for the Florida Citrus Commission and started commuting.

It was decided the rebellious Lee should attend St. Leo's Preparatory School, near Dade City, Florida. He managed to stick it out for a year and a half, but the United States's getting into World War II coincided nicely with Lee and his prep school having had enough of each other. After a total of three years of high school, he stopped attending classes—again.

Lee had decided he belonged in the Marines. No doubt he would be killed anyway, so he would go out with the toughest, the bravest, the most valiant of fighting men. Lamont was in full accord with this judgment, and, at age fifty-one, he joined up himself. Back with the U.S. Army, Lamont helped set up antiaircraft gun emplacements in

England that destroyed a number of German V-2 rockets during the war. This time he was to return home as a first sergeant, with yet more decorations.

Lee enlisted in the Marine Corps on 12 August 1942 in New York City. He was shipped off to recruit camp at Parris Island, and then on to the 4th Separate Recruit Battalion Training Center at the Marine base in New River, North Carolina. With Robert having enlisted in the Army Air Corps, Courtenay was left alone with her job in New York to coolly reflect on how she had wound up as the queen of this clan of fierce warriors.

Lee was in top physical shape, thanks to the one scholastic activity he did enjoy—athletics. He shot sharpshooter in boot camp, missing expert by one point. Later he talked his way into administrative work by convincing his drill instructor that he knew how to type, which he did not. Next he was sent to Quartermaster School at New River, where he was promoted to corporal. Lee Marvin was then ordered to Service Company, Marine Barracks at Camp Elliot, San Diego, California. He was eighteen years old.

A few minor scrapes at Elliot got him demoted to private, after which he was placed in a Casual Company in the 4th Marine Division, readying itself for combat. Marvin underwent demolitions training with B Company, 20th Marine Engineer Battalion. Five months later his senior officers had had their fill of his offensive behavior; Marvin was ordered to mess duty for over a month. But the boredom would not last: soon enough he would find himself in the middle of a brutal war.

In January 1944, Marvin shipped out as part of D Company, 4th Tank Battalion (Scout-Snipers), Headquarters Battalion, 4th Marine Division. (In March 1944, the unit was redesignated as a reconnaissance company.) He was bound for the Marshall Islands. Thirty-two atolls formed these two island chains, which held two major Japanese bases—Eniwetok and Kwajalein.

Marvin, whose group was with the 22d Marines, was part of a divisional reconnaissance company. Sent in the night before the attack for reconnaissance on Kwajalein, Marvin told author Donald Zec: "If you were fired on you were supposed to throw a poncho over your head,

Private Marvin with a Japanese light machine gun (Nambu Type 96). (Robert Filkosky and Lester Jeurgenson, USMC)

whip out a blue flashlight and draw an X on the map where the fire was coming from." (This and the Marvin quotes that follow, used with permission, are from Zec, *Marvin: The Story of Lee Marvin*, 36–40.)

> Well, I don't think anybody actually threw a poncho over their head, and nobody fired back either. Because once you fired you . . . were . . . dead! Of course we'd all get miserably lost and screwed up. The next morning—if you got that far—the sun would come up and there would be the whole United States Navy out there because it's D-Day and they would be shelling you because if they saw you they figured you were Japs and nobody told them otherwise. So, God, it was absolute confusion. You're hit by friend and foe. So you eventually swim out to a reef and pray; and hope Goddamit, that somebody's listening.

Once the Marines had taken Eniwetok and Kwajalein, Marvin was sent on R and R to Maui, Hawaii, where he was also trained for his next foray. This was to be with I Company, 3d Battalion, 24th

Marines, 4th Marine Division. Next stop, Saipan in the Marianas, 15 June 1944.

We went in on Yellow Beach Two. It was morning. The first day. . . . We clawed forward and hit the basic scrub of the beach. Beyond it were those big open fields, thousands of sticks with saki bottles on top. My assumptions then were they were used as insulators for wires that had been knocked down. But I was wrong. The Japs were using them as artillery markers. They had us nicely pinpointed on a checker-board. They didn't miss. . . . The artillery got very bad, and all the bombing was coming down real heavy. We finally got to a very large trench, about, I'd say eight hundred yards inland. There was really a tremendous downpour of this stuff so we all bailed into the trench, and we were sitting there, you know, thanking God for this kind of cover when I noticed the parapets of the trenches forward of us had firing slits and it dawned on me they belonged to them not us. I happened to say this when they started opening up at us all along the trench. We bailed out and went forward, thinking it would be better forward than backwards and they just cleaned out that trench and it must have been three thousand yards long.

Some of them survived until that night, by which time, Marvin estimated, a mere thirty yards separated them from the enemy.

We lost quite a few that night. But the next day we pushed towards Aslito airfield [renamed Isely Field after its capture]. We got pinned down there and lost some more guys going through those cane fields. We were pulled out and on the fourth morning we were heading up into what was later called "Death Valley" and it looked it. We had to push up this mountain Tapotchau [an extinct volcano, rough limestone most of the way up to its summit at 1,554 feet]. Well the mountain looked okay. I mean if you lived that long you could probably get to the top. Looked simple really. But nobody could get far enough to lick the bastard. . . . They sent our company in. . . .

So then the Captain shouted to fall in but I couldn't get in myself. We'd just got into one knot, caught dead in an ambush, and Jesus Christ it was just decimation. We had started out with 247 men and fifteen minutes later there were six of us. "I" Company. Third Battalion, 24th Marines. Six fellers. So anyway it was my turn to get

Two Marines take cover in a shell hole on Saipan, June 1944.

nailed. There are two prominent parts of your body in view to the enemy when you flatten out—your head and your ass. If you present one, you get killed. If you raise the other, you get shot in the ass. I got shot in the ass.

Twenty-seven gun emplacements were discovered around them the day after this ferocious action, as Lee and other survivors crawled out as best they could. But the hell was not over yet.

So then, Jesus, they start bringing the other guys out and we had a guy called Calello who had been hit in the back of the skull. . . . So he was kinda screaming you know and they were trying to get him out of there, hollering for stretcher-bearers. But there weren't any and finally one did come so they got Calello on. While they were putting him on, one of the bearers got killed with a one-shot, another one got knocked right through the back killing him too, and Calello got a bullet in the hip. Calello got hit three times while he was being put on a stretcher. He was a screaming mess, you can understand that. And one guy ran by me and stepped right on my ass. I mean right on the thing. It was a big hole which I found out later was nine-by-three-by-three just lying open but I was alive and still had my .45 automatic which gave me some blast if I needed it.

Marvin was given morphine and placed with the other "savable" wounded men. He had just gulped down some water offered to him from a plasma can when "the whole world went WOOM! About a hundred and fifty yards in front of us one of the Japanese dumps we'd captured had been hit and you looked up and you could see those marines flying through the air, slowly. . . ."

Marvin was blown off his stretcher and landed squarely on his lacerated behind. He heard some screaming about a counterattack but was powerless to assist or even defend himself—he'd given his pistol away. Meanwhile the wounded were being carried back to the beach, and Marvin and another casualty were put in a jeep. Off they charged —into enemy-held territory. Reeling around as soon as they realized their mistake, they made it back to the beach. By now it was a far from peaceful evening, with shell fire roaring all around, dead bodies everywhere, fellow Marines being blown into the air, Japanese soldiers moving and firing from behind trees and parapets.

Marvin had stopped bleeding, but it was looking as if he was going to have to spend the night on that beach. Then they managed to load him into a passing LCM (landing craft, medium). He was taken out to the hospital ship *Solace*. There, lulled by faint strains of "Moonlight Serenade" and morphine, against a background of gunfire on the deadly shoreline from which he'd just been rescued, Lee Marvin realized that he was finally safe but others were not, and the tears began to come. The nightmares would come for the rest of his life.

Wounded in action on 18 June 1944, Marvin spent the next thirteen months in naval hospitals, under treatment for his laceration and a severed sciatic nerve. In a hospital on Guadalcanal, he was awarded the Purple Heart medal. He also later received a Presidential Unit Citation, Letter of Commendation with Ribbon, Asiatic-Pacific Area Campaign Medal, American Area Campaign Medal, and World War II Victory Medal.

In the Boston naval hospital, after being informed that he'd escaped being permanently paralyzed by a hair's breadth, he was released. Lee

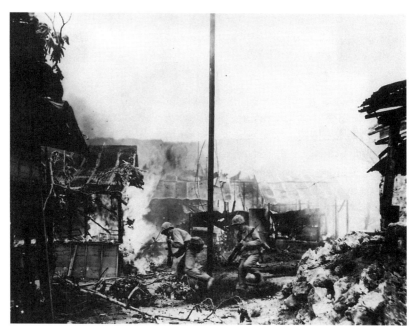

Supporting infantry and artillery set Japanese installations ablaze as Marine infantrymen enter Garapan, Saipan's main city, July 1944.

Marvin was discharged on 24 July 1945 at the Marine Barracks, Philadelphia, with a small disability pension.

Soon he was reunited with his brother, back from England and Belgium, and his father, back for the second time from a war-torn Europe. The warriors were bewildered and depressed now that they found themselves out of action, and a few months later Lamont had a total breakdown. Courtenay promptly abandoned her professional pursuits and moved the family to Woodstock, New York, which was to remain their permanent base of operations.

Lee worked at various odd jobs and took a typing and shorthand course. He cut grass, shoveled snow, and finally became a plumber's assistant, but not before trying unsuccessfully to re-up in the Marines. He could not because of his disability, it was gently explained to him.

It was through mowing lawns and fixing toilets that Lee Marvin eventually found his way into the movies. His lawn-mowing business had taken him weekly to the grounds of one of the area's doctors,

Marines throw hand grenades at an enemy position on Saipan, July 1944.

who'd taken a liking to the young war veteran and begun inviting him along on fishing outings. These expeditions introduced Marvin to the man who ran Woodstock's Maverick Theater.

One day Marvin was called in to work on the theater's backed-up toilet. From his post in the washroom, he could hear the exciting hustle and bustle of a rehearsal getting under way. His job completed, he wandered into the auditorium and was immediately spellbound. The tension in the air, the togetherness, the focused team work . . . it all reminded him of the Marines. This was for him. And, as it happened, the director had asked the manager to find him a tall, loud man to fill in for a sick actor. Lee Marvin got the job.

He went on to formal training at the American Theater Wing, New York, courtesy of the GI Bill. From 1948 to 1950 he played small roles off Broadway, appeared on live television, and toured with theater productions. He also appeared on Broadway, in *Billy Budd.* In 1950 the director of the movie *You're in the Navy Now* (1951), shot partly in

Norfolk, Virginia, was sufficiently impressed by the way Marvin delivered his few lines to take him back to Hollywood, where he appeared in other scenes. The director also introduced Lee Marvin to an agent with whom he developed a lasting—and lucrative for both parties—business relationship.

In 1952 Marvin married Betty Ebeling. The wild one stayed with her for fourteen often-happy, often-difficult years, fathering four children. Divorced in 1965, Marvin married a second time four years later. Pamela Feeley had been a heartthrob back in Woodstock, after the war. Rekindling the flame twenty-five years later, they were married in 1970.

He gave up his longtime party scene at Malibu, with which he had grown weary anyway, and in 1975 he and Pam settled on a twenty-acre ranch near Tucson, Arizona. Marvin had by this time cut back significantly on his legendary alcohol intake as he had begun—finally—to prefer the calmer joys of domesticity.

Before ending his relationship with Michelle Triola, with whom he lived from 1964 to 1970 but whom he never married, Lee tried a second time to re-enlist in the Marines. After a particularly unpleasant disagreement with Michelle, he left the house and, downing a few invigorating shots, made his way over to Camp Pendleton. From there Michelle got an official-sounding but understanding phone call, requesting that she come and collect him.

When Lee married Pamela, Michelle sued and claimed half of his fortune. Her "palimony" suit became a landmark case, calling under scrutiny the rights of someone who has been abandoned after living as if married but without the protection of the legal document. After much court wrangling, in 1979 the judge ruled that Michelle had failed to demonstrate that there had been a contract between Lee and herself. Nevertheless, he ordered Marvin to pay her $104,000 to cover the costs of her readjustment from living as if she were Mrs. Marvin to a simpler, but independent, existence. Michelle accepted the ruling.

Rocky terrain in his personal life had not prevented Lee Marvin from rising to uncontested stardom. He played in some forty films and starred in the TV police adventure series *M Squad*, which paved the way for later shows such as *Columbo* and *Kojak*. He also made television appearances on the *Dick Powell Theater*, the *Schlitz Playhouse*, *Route 66*, *Twilight Zone*, *Suspense Theater*, and *Desilu Playhouse*.

In his early roles he was typecast as the heavy, rough, tough guy, often a villain. Later he was able to display more complex abilities, and he won the best-actor Academy Award for his dual performance in the film *Cat Ballou* (1965). Other memorable films include *The Big Heat* (1953), *The Wild One* (1953), *Bad Day at Black Rock* (1955), *The Comancheros* (1961), *The Man Who Shot Liberty Valance* (1962), *Ship of Fools* (1965), *Hell in the Pacific* (1968), *The Iceman Cometh* (1973), and *Gorky Park* (1983).

Predictably, he was quite at home in the role of a military man. Marvin got to act in several films with former Marines. One of his finest characters was the steely-eyed Major Reisman in the classic war movie *The Dirty Dozen* (1967), in which Marvin was part actor, part ex-Marine reliving history. He was not alone, costarring with Robert Ryan, ex-Marine; Robert Webber, ex-Marine; Ernest Borgnine, ex-Navy; and Charles Bronson, ex-Army.

In 1978, filming began for *The Big Red One* (1979). Lee Marvin played a crusty, battle-experienced sergeant, and seeing immediately that his actor-soldiers had no idea how to handle their weapons, he undertook their training himself. Off the set, he had the actors fire blanks while he acquired M-1 rifles and ammunition. Now he could begin full-fledged target practice. Next he added nomenclature to the curriculum, with instruction in how to break down and clean the rifles. After a couple of months Sergeant Marvin had the actors in shape, and they handled their weapons on screen the way Marines would do it in real life. He even had them taking the rifles home at night to clean them.

Lee Marvin's love affair with the Corps lasted all his life. A year before his death at age sixty-three, in an interview for the Marine Corps magazine *Leatherneck* (July 1986, 35), he said, "When I see a young Marine in the airport, I think about how this guy is getting his presence together—that boot camp is doing its job. There's a mettle to him standing in the airport wearing that uniform with his rifle badge. Yeah, I guess I see myself."

He is buried at Arlington National Cemetery near the Tomb of the Unknown Soldier, beside world heavyweight boxing champion Joe Louis. His headstone is inscribed: "Lee Marvin, PFC, U.S. Marine Corps, World War II, Feb. 19 1924–Aug. 29 1987."

Saipan

The outer ring of Japanese defenses was breached in November 1943 and early 1944, when the Marines took Tarawa and the Marines-Army captured Kwajalein and Eniwetok atolls. These conquests opened the way for the invasion of inner-ring island defenses, linked by Saipan, Tinian, and Guam. The new islands lay within air-striking distance of Japan, and their capture was given highest priority in the Central Pacific Drive toward the Japanese home islands.

It took from 15 June to 9 July 1944 to secure Saipan. Though brutal and costly in American lives (3,225 killed, 13,061 wounded, 326 missing in action), it was devastating for the enemy, with 23,811 confirmed dead and 736 prisoners. It was one of the most decisive victories in the Pacific. After it, Japanese generals and admirals sensed that their war was lost, and the Americans drove that point home by also wresting Tinian and Guam from Japanese control.

Soon after the capture of Saipan, B-29 Superfortresses flying from Saipan and Tinian began a continuous air campaign against Japan. But it would be another year before World War II ended—a year during which the Philippines were recaptured and U.S. Marines fought the bloody battles for Peleliu, Iwo Jima, and Okinawa, the costliest, for them, of the entire war.

Peter J. Ortiz

W hile Sterling Hayden joined in the support of Yugoslav partisans in the eastern Mediterranean, other Marines attached to the OSS performed similar hazardous duty in
eastern Europe. Few in number and assigned high-risk covert missions,
these Marines fought with the same courage and esprit de corps as
their fellow Marines in the Pacific. Among them was French Foreign
Legion–trained Maj. Pierre "Peter" Ortiz, a man who displayed an
unrelenting fearlessness that amazed all those around him. By the war's
end, Ortiz was the most decorated U.S. military man to have served
with the OSS.

Born in New York City on 5 July 1913, Pierre Julien Ortiz was
raised in affluence. He was the son of prestigious French-Spanish pub-
lisher Philippe George Julien Ortiz and his wife, Marie Louise, born
in Switzerland, whose own mother was Russian. With this interna-

(Jean Morlan collection)

Ortiz served in the French Foreign Legion and fought the Berbers in Morocco, where he later returned as a U.S. Marine. His specialty: one-man reconnaissance behind enemy lines. (National Archives)

tional background, the young Ortiz was sent to a lycée in France, from where he was to go on to attend a university in either Europe or the States.

But in January 1932, the multilingual youth astonished and dismayed his family by suddenly leaving school and traveling to Sidi-bel-Abbès, where he joined the 1st Regiment of the Foreign Legion. The nineteen-year-old, six-foot-three-inch, natural athlete, who enjoyed running, climbing mountains, and riding horses, wanted to "live a man's life," he told G. Ward Price, who interviewed him on Mount Hamdoun in 1932 or 1933 for his book *In Morocco with the Legion.*

Philippe immediately followed his impetuous son to Africa, to save him from what he perceived to be a potentially fatal mistake. A Legion marshal understood the father's concerns and assured him that an "irregular" enlistment could, indeed, be canceled. But in the end, the Legion won Philippe over too. After he had spent some time observing its workings, he traveled all over Morocco and Algeria to learn more about it. When he returned to Paris, he founded Les Amis de la Légion Etrangère, "Friends of the Foreign Legion," in the hopes of promoting a better understanding of the organization and its function, history, and interior workings, and to assist legionnaires when they reentered the civilian world.

In fact, Philippe discovered, men were not routinely killed for minor offenses in the Foreign Legion; rather, official disciplinary measures were much like those of any other service—even if, perhaps, administered for lesser infractions. And the enlistees were not all criminals, but were rather mostly strong and independent men, unafraid of danger, who sought an alternative to the lack of gainful employment in their respective countries.

The Legion's goal was to train tough men to survive in the field, alone, for weeks at a time, if necessary. In a country short on water and long on deserts, in-garrison discipline may have been rigorous, but while on campaign, sandals and even marching in one's underwear were tolerated. To get rid of extra weight, legionnaires often sold or disposed of boots or other articles of clothing, and replacing these with native garb was a common and accepted practice, as was a more loose, informal relationship between officers and men.

Ortiz served five years as a legionnaire, graduating from its parachute course and fighting the Berbers (who were seeking independence from France) in Morocco. In 1934 he was promoted to sergeant, becoming the youngest noncommissioned officer in the Legion. His service completed, he returned home to his family, who had by this time relocated to La Jolla, California.

But when Germany invaded Poland on 1 September 1939, and England and France declared war on Germany on 3 September, Pierre Ortiz could not bring himself to stay out of it. He sailed from Canada in October—the Germans torpedoed his ship, and he made it the rest of the way on a French destroyer—and rejoined the Legion.

He was commissioned a second lieutenant, and he fought for two years before his regiment was overrun by German forces. Ortiz, severely wounded, was taken prisoner and sent to a concentration camp in Austria, where German surgeons patched him up. He promptly began a series of escape attempts, finally succeeding and making his way to Portugal in October 1941. From there he was able to return to California to convalesce.

The Pearl Harbor attack occurred shortly after his arrival, and the United States officially joined the Allied fight against the Axis. Because of Ortiz's wounds, no American military service would accept him for duty, so he had to spend several months healing and getting back into shape before he was able to pass the Marine Corps physical.

Peter Ortiz joined the Marines in June 1942 and was sent to Parris Island for boot training—not as hard, he later remarked, as what he'd gone through in the Legion. It was clear from the start that he was not a typical recruit when he appeared in formation wearing several French decorations for valor, which were validated when Headquarters, Marine Corps, made inquiries. After Parris Island, Ortiz was given parachute training and directly commissioned as a Reserve second lieutenant.

He was sent to Morocco, where he organized a patrol of Arab tribesmen who scouted German forces on the Tunisian front. Ortiz himself was disguised as a tribesman, and with his dark looks and facility with local Arabic languages, it was his own people who represented the greatest threat. The Americans shot at him, captured him, and did not believe that he was a U.S. Marine. Finally he was able to convince an Army officer of his identity and mission.

On a subsequent assignment, with a British light armored reconnaissance unit against Germany's 21st Panzer Division, Ortiz was shot in the hand and leg one night while conducting a one-man reconnaissance. But he managed to keep his enemies at bay with the help of his grenades, and made it back to his unit.

After he had recovered, Peter Ortiz was promoted to captain, assigned to the OSS, and sent to southeastern France's Haute Savoie department, to the thirty-by-twelve-mile Vercors plateau. Rising to three thousand feet above sea level, this rugged region is covered by a large forest, a natural fortress that in late 1943 was inhabited by bears, farmers, and three thousand Free French maquisards.

Gen. Charles de Gaulle, the British Special Operations Executive (SOE), and the American OSS were aware of the maquisards' presence—and of the fact that French Resistance fighters could be of tremendous worth, if they could be properly armed and trained. The invasion of Europe was by this time a strong possibility; in-country guerrilla forces harassing enemy troops behind the lines could prove disastrous for German soldiers faced with a frontal assault as well as hit-and-run operations to their rear.

The Vercors plateau offered a unique staging base from which maquisard raiding parties could attack the enemy, but arming and training the Free French force would prove difficult. The Allied elite fighting forces considered the risks worth taking, and together they conceived a scheme to join forces with the maquis in their fight against the Germans, while at the same time inspiring the rest of the Alpine population to rise against the occupation force.

Carrying out the plan required close cooperation between the best talent available. An Allied team of three was formed for the mission, code-named Union. They were H. H. A. Thackwaite, a noted British clandestine warrior; "Monnier," an experienced and gifted French radio operator; and Peter J. Ortiz, U.S. Marine captain and former decorated French legionnaire. Five months before Overlord, their mission was to scope out the capabilities of maquis units, determining if they had the leadership and fighting ability to effectively harass the German occupation forces during and after the invasion of Europe.

On the moonless night of 6 January 1944, the three parachuted from a Royal Air Force bomber. Per standard SOE operation procedure, they wore civilian clothes. However, after they met the maquis they changed into their uniforms, in a clear statement that this was to be a full military operation.

They found several large maquis groups ready to fight, but insufficiently armed and trained. Additionally, there were several different factions, who often disagreed as to ideology, loyalties, and appropriate methods to be employed. Monnier, Ortiz, and Thackwaite took the time required to evaluate the situation thoroughly, reporting regularly back to London by radio.

Ortiz liked to gather intelligence on his own, walking into German-occupied towns in civilian clothing. He would stop in cafés and listen to the local talk, which he understood whether it was in French or German. One time, he happened to sit down next to German soldiers who were talking about the irritating maquis and the hated Americans who were working with them. This was more than Ortiz could bear. He stood up, threw open his cape, and, pointing his two .45 automatics at them, watched as they carried out his command to raise a toast to President Franklin Roosevelt and the United States Marine Corps. He then melted into the darkness outside.

Ortiz was a master thief, a useful skill that he drew upon as needed. Obtaining a Gestapo pass, he stole German vehicles almost at will. When four downed Royal Air Force aviators needed help, it was Ortiz who accompanied them to the Spanish border and freedom.

Out of the chaos, Union eventually succeeded in organizing separate Resistance groups into effective fighting forces, and the maquis threat to the Germans grew greater. The Resistance fighters began to expand their harassment operations into areas the Germans had thought secure. The latter countered with three Panzer Grenadier battalions that attacked the Vercors plateau in February 1944, successfully sealing it off. The French fought valiantly but lacked heavy guns, ammunition, and other support equipment to hold off a superior force. Thus they were forced to fight on the defensive, staging hit-and-run raids when possible.

By May, Union planners had agreed that a much more concerted effort would have to be launched as quickly as possible. Monnier, Ortiz, and Thackwaite were extracted, and a few weeks later two new missions, Justine and Eucalyptus, were air-dropped into the area.

On 6 June 1944, the Allies invaded Normandy. In the Vercors

region, the fighting intensified. On 19 July, the Germans assaulted the town of Vassieux with glider-borne troops. The French put up a ferocious defense, but the town fell and was destroyed. The Germans rounded up and shot civilians who survived the ordeal.

With Allied armies pushing inland at Normandy, the Haute Savoie fighting continued. The Wehrmacht was gaining the upper hand, and Allied higher command determined that another Union mission was in order. Union II represented a new type of OSS mission: Operational Groups (OGs), formed to carry out direct action against the Germans. This included sabotage and taking over critical sites to prevent the retreating enemy from destroying them. The heavily armed OGs, the most militarized of OSS units, operated in uniform at all times. On 1 August 1944, B-17 Flying Fortresses of the U.S. Army Air Corps's 388th Heavy Bomb Group took off from Knettershall Airfield, England. Maj. Peter Ortiz, carrying a million francs for the Resistance, was put in charge of Union II. He led five other U.S. Marines (Gy. Sgt. Robert LaSalle and Sgts. John Bodnar, Fred Brunner, Charles Perry, and Jack Risler), Free French officer Joseph Arcelin (code-named Jo-Jo and carrying the faked papers of a Marine sergeant), and U.S. Army Air Corps captain Francis Coolidge. These men parachuted into a drop zone near the town of Beaufort, bringing 864 containers of supplies for the French Bulle Battalion, located in the Col d'Arecle.

When their B-17 bomber swooped in over the Alps at low altitude and arrived at its drop zone, the team quickly filed out a rear hatchway. Their parachutes were yanked open by cables attached to the plane. Unfortunately, Sergeant Perry's cable snapped and he fell to his death. The French in the surrounding area never forgot the heroics of the team, and after the war they erected a monument carrying the inscription, "In Memory of American Sergeant Charles Perry, fallen on the field of honor in the act of parachuting."

After this depressing start, Union II spent its first few weeks training the French guerrillas in the use and maintenance of their new weapons, and planning where to strike the enemy. Ortiz and his men went to Beaufort and made contact with the Forces Françaises de l'Intérieur. They then moved on to Montgirod, where the Germans shelled them from nearby hills as they entered the town.

Forced to take to the surrounding mountains as the Germans took

Standing at attention over the grave of their lost comrade Sgt. Charles E. Perry, USMC, in the French Alps at Col-des Saises are *(from left)*: Maj. Peter J. Ortiz, USMC; Capt. Francis Coolidge, Army Air Corps; Gy. Sgt. Robert LaSalle, USMC; Sgt. John P. Bodnar, USMC; Sgt. Frederick J. Brunner, USMC; and Sgt. Jack Risler, USMC.

bloody revenge on the town, the Union II force hid out with the Bulle Battalion. Robert LaSalle had fallen ill and developed a high fever, and they left him hidden in the mountains under the care of a priest who spoke some English.

They had to stay on the move because of the Germans on their tail, who eventually surrounded them. But the Allies were trapped in an area full of gullies and canyons, and in the twilight, Ortiz and his men were able to crawl through enemy lines. Meanwhile Operation Anvil, the Allied invasion of southern France, had just begun. German forces were starting to move, and Union II found a German-free village, Longefoy, willing to feed and shelter them for one night. Then, on 16 August 1944, Union II arrived in Centron.

Marching in single file with full packs on their backs, the group made it through the town. But just on the other side of Centron, they ran into a German motorized convoy. Enemy troops jumped from the vehicles and opened fire. At the same time, armored cars began pouring machine-gun fire at the dispersing group. Brunner and Coolidge dove into a river and escaped. Ortiz and the others retreated back into Centron, where house-to-house fighting ensued. By now a force of just four—Arcelin, Bodnar, Risler, and Ortiz—was holding off an enemy battalion.

But the townspeople told them that Centron would get the same treatment as Montgirod had received—or worse—unless the Allies surrendered. Ortiz knew that the Germans were brutal against towns that harbored the maquis, and that Centron would probably be destroyed and its citizens shot. He ordered the others to escape while it was still possible, but they would not leave him alone.

Under a white flag, Ortiz negotiated with the German battalion commander: he and his men would surrender if the town and its people were spared. The commander, Major Kolb, agreed, and he kept his word. After their surrender, Arcelin did make an escape attempt, but he was quickly recaptured.

Brunner made it from the river back to where LaSalle was hiding, and he filled him in on recent developments. The two moved out immediately and took separate routes to safety, LaSalle heading south. He eventually reached Anvil forces who were moving northward; Brunner made it to England within a few weeks.

The other OSS men were imprisoned at the naval POW camp Marlag/Milag Nord in the German burg of Westertimke, outside Bremen. On the way there, Ortiz made repeated escape attempts, in return for which he got some predictably rough treatment. However, fortunately for the Marines, Marlag/Milag was one of the more hospitable stalags, where, aside from searches and regular roll calls, the German guards contented themselves with making sure their prisoners stayed inside the wire.

Escape attempts had previously been forbidden among the officers, but Ortiz promptly proclaimed himself the senior American POW who would set his own rules. He began to plan for escape, with Navy lieutenant (jg) Hiram Harris. Ortiz's first attempt, on 18 December 1944, involved over an hour of cutting through several wires. After Ortiz made it through to the open field outside the compound, a patrol snagged Harris, sounded the alarm, and turned the searchlights on

Ortiz. The two were roughed up (again, at least for Ortiz) and placed in solitary confinement.

Two months later, in February, Ortiz began planning again, this time with 2d Lt. Walter W. Taylor, USMCR, another OSS man. Through the black-market network that had been operating within and near the camp, the prisoners were able to learn that the Allies were getting ever closer. Ortiz and Taylor began stockpiling supplies—maps, food, clothes, anything they could get. But on 10 April, the commandant abruptly ordered the prisoners to prepare to move. Within three hours they were walking toward the port city of Lubeck, which was at least eight days to the north.

In the confusion of the hasty departure, many of the POWs were able to hide within the camp. But the Germans kept a close watch on Ortiz, who walked out with the rest of the column. They walked for three hours before RAF Spitfires attacked. As the planes began shooting and all semblance of order broke loose, Ortiz, Taylor, Air Corps lieutenant Donald McNaughton, and Royal Marines warrant officer Stancombe ran into the woods, kept going for a bit, and then fell silent, waiting. The survivors of the column moved on without them.

But the Allies did not, as expected, follow shortly, and for ten days the little group hid by day and walked by night, blindly searching for the British lines they believed must be somewhere nearby. Several times they stumbled into trouble but managed to get away, and eventually they made their way back to Westertimke. Here the sick, weak group, after reconnoitering the situation within the camp, decided they would be better off back inside their huts and fed, warmed with blankets, than outside and free but soon dead—especially since there were only a few guards left, and the POWs were virtually running the compound.

On 28 April 1945, the prisoners at Marlag Nord heard bagpipes— it was the 1st Scottish Armored Division. The Allies had finally reached Marlag Nord, and the camp was officially liberated. Most POWs gratefully boarded trucks bound for the rear. But four U.S. Marines— Ortiz, Taylor, Risler, and Bodnar—presented themselves to the officer in charge, requesting to join his unit in order to "bag a few more Germans before hunting season closed" (Robert E. Mattingly, "Who Knew Not Fear," n. 20. Quoted from Maj. Peter J. Ortiz, "Chronological Report of the Capture and Subsequent Captivity of Members of Mission Union," 13 May 1945).

The repatriation officer did not think this would be a wise move, and instead he sent the weakened men to staging areas behind the front. Ortiz was evacuated to Brussels. Reporting to OSS headquarters there, he asked for more combat duty, but the war ended while Ortiz was in California being prepared for a mission in Indochina.

For his service in Europe with the OSS, the French made the "hero of the Haute Savoie" a member of the Legion of Honor and awarded him the Croix de Guerre (two palms, gold star, silver star, and five citations), the Croix de Combattants, the Ouissam Alouite, and the Médaille Coloniale. The British made him an Officer of the Most Excellent Order of the British Empire. The Americans awarded him with a Navy Cross with gold star in lieu of a second Navy Cross, the Legion of Merit, and two Purple Hearts. His gold star citation reads:

> For extraordinary heroism while serving with the Office of Strategic Services during operations behind enemy Axis lines in the Savoie Department of France, from 1 August 1944 to 27 April 1945. After parachuting into a region where his activities had made him an object of intensive search by the Gestapo, Major Ortiz valiantly continued his work in coordinating and leading resistance groups in that section. When he and his team were attacked and surrounded during a special mission designed to immobilize enemy reinforcements stationed in that area, he disregarded the possibility of escape and, in an effort to spare villagers severe reprisals by the Gestapo, surrendered to the sadistic Geheim Staats Polizei. Subsequently imprisoned and subjected to numerous interrogations, he divulged nothing, and the story of this intrepid Marine Major and his team has become a brilliant legend in that section of France where acts of bravery were considered commonplace. By his outstanding loyalty and self-sacrificing devotion to duty, Major Ortiz contributed materially to the success of operations against a relentless enemy, and upheld the highest traditions of the United States Naval Service.

Ortiz returned to civilian life in 1946, becoming active in the Marine Corps Reserve after the war. In California, he worked as a technical and dialogue consultant in the movie industry, often with director John Ford, another former OSS man with whom he became close friends. In 1948 he married Jean Morlan, with whom he had one son (Lt. Col. Peter J. Ortiz, Jr., USMC). Eventually they settled in Arizona, where Ortiz enjoyed his many interests, ranging from art, history, and religion to Hollywood.

Two movies were made that mirrored his wartime escapades: *13 Rue Madelaine* (1946, starring James Cagney) and *Operation Secret* (1952, starring Cornel Wilde). Ortiz was the technical adviser on these films. Peter Ortiz also found work as an actor, appearing in *Twelve O'Clock High* (1949), *Spy Hunt* (1950), *When Willie Comes Marching Home* (1950), *Sirocco* (1951), *Retreat Hell* (1952), *Jubilee Train* (1954), *King Richard and the Crusaders* (1954), *Son of Sinbad* (1955) *Seventh Cavalry* (1956), and the John Wayne movies *Rio Grande* (1950) and *The Wings of Eagles* (1957).

Known to all as a polite, compassionate man who had striven to set a good example for the Marines who served under him, Renaissance man Col. Peter J. Ortiz, USMCR (Ret.), died in 1988. He was buried with full military honors at Arlington National Cemetery, with representatives of the British and French governments present.

The people of Centron still honor the four men who saved their town. In the mayor's office, a plaque is inscribed: "In memory of the passage of Commander Ortiz and his valiant companions, 16th August 1944." On 1 August 1992, Centron named the town center Place Peter Ortiz. Among the many attendees at the ceremony were retired Sgt. Maj. John P. Bodnar and former sergeant Jack R. Risler.

PART 2

Semper Fidelis

Bob Burns

In the late 1930s and early 1940s, radio and movie comic Bob Burns was known especially for his amusing musical invention, the bazooka. Made of two metal tubes that fit into one another, sliding like a trombone, this contraption was played by vibrating one's lips while blowing into the opening where the mouthpiece would normally be. Working the "slide" at the same time created variations in tone, and the whole effect blasted into the world through a soldered-on funnel at the other end.

By the time Burns returned from Europe after World War I, the bazooka had become his trademark. The U.S. Army commandeered the name in 1943, to designate its World War II light portable antitank rocket launcher—which looked a lot like Burns's well-known bazooka.

Born on 2 August 1891 in Van Buren, Arkansas, Bob Burns came

(Photofest)

from a farming area. His father was a civil engineer who supported his family comfortably enough for young Bob to take mandolin lessons, while his brother studied guitar. Both boys took to music making, which they pursued on their own with their friends, for fun.

One evening in 1905, when Bob was fourteen, he and a few others were practicing in the back of a plumbing-supply store, when Bob picked up two pieces of pipe. It was the beginning of his invention, so named because blowing one's "bazoo," in Van Buren, Arkansas, meant talking too much. Soon young Burns was playing the instrument at dances, where revelers loved his surprisingly simple entertainment. It would take him far beyond local balls. In 1907 it got him into the Black Cat Minstrels' show in Fort Smith, Arkansas, and in 1911 he took it into vaudeville, traveling through his home state and through Oklahoma, Texas, and Louisiana. His brother came down too, with his guitar, and the two played in theaters throughout New Orleans, then decided to take the act to New York.

They had to stop periodically to refurbish their resources. Their detours took them to Norfolk, Virginia, where they worked on board a passenger ship for a few months, supplementing their pay with entertainment for the more well-heeled travelers. Eventually they left the ship at Baltimore and picked up odd jobs for a while, after which they finally made it to New York.

But soon they parted ways, Bob's brother moving on to St. Louis to accept a job offer. In 1913 Bob found work as an extra for New York's Biograph Company Motion Picture Studio, but before long he hit the road again. He traveled around the country working at yet more odd jobs—farm hand, construction worker, and, when he could, vaudeville. At some point, following in his father's footsteps, he studied to be a civil engineer at the University of Arkansas.

But putting his degree to use would have to wait a while, until Bob Burns had satisfied his hankering for wandering and show business. The bazooka was always with him; if he lost it, he went to a pipe fitter and had another one made for under three dollars.

Burns joined the Marine Corps in Chicago in 1917, bazooka in hand. He went through boot camp at Parris Island, where, on the shooting range, he held the highest grades for marksmanship in the regiment. He had enjoyed squirrel shooting as a boy, and the Marines quickly noted his skills and put them to work. Burns was made a gunnery instructor and retained at Parris Island for seventeen more months, during which he took part in the championship matches at Camp Perry, Ohio.

World War I seemed a long way off. To entertain themselves and perhaps earn a little extra dough, Burns and his buddies formed a jazz band and played at camp dances and officers' parties. But before long the Marine Jazz Band was shipped overseas, on board the transport *DeKalb* (No. 3010), formerly the German ship *Prinz Eitel Friedrich.* The ship had put into Norfolk on 11 March 1915 but had not left port in the time allowed by international law. Interned and moved to Philadelphia when the United States entered the war, U.S. Customs seized her and transferred her to the Navy, where she was renamed.

Burns and the jazz band never did see the trenches in which so many lost their lives in France: the armistice had been signed before they stepped off the *DeKalb* at Brest. But they did sleep in military-issue

Between performances at Camp Pendleton, 1944, Bob Burns plays a few notes on the bazooka for comedienne Cass Daly and Marines.

pup tents in the French mud near Brest, and they did see plenty of a more pleasurable sort of action. As they entertained troops throughout the country, Bob Burns's bazooka became an international phenomenon.

The band was ordered to join the 11th Marine Regiment, which, in an interview for *Leatherneck* (June 1944), Burns dubbed the "shootingest outfit in the Marines." He was right at home in that department: he became one of 1,400 finalists in the rifle and pistol championships of the American Expeditionary Forces. In the end, gunnery sergeant Bob Burns finished high man in rapid fire and was awarded the division champion's gold medal.

Upon his return from Europe and following his discharge from the Corps, Burns returned to his old pattern of moving from job to job. A big man of ruddy complexion, calm demeanor, and deliberate, witty speech, he toured the East Coast running concession stands. In time this occupation took him to Atlantic City, where he met his first wife, Elizabeth Fisher, on the boardwalk. She, too, was a concession-stand entrepreneur.

Together they opened an Atlantic City dance hall, which folded a few months later. They traveled on the vaudeville circuit for eight years, and when the market crashed in 1929, Bob was in a blackface act. But the crash meant the end of vaudeville; the Burnses found themselves in need of another way to produce income.

Hearing that Twentieth-Century Fox was interested in the blackface act, they rushed to New York for a screen test. They were signed to a year's contract, and Bob and Elizabeth Burns packed up their son and drove out to California.

A few years of lackluster work followed, until, in 1932, Burns found a job in radio. He began spinning his famous tall tales about people back in the Ozarks, such as Uncle Fud and Grandpaw Snazzy. In 1935 Rudy Vallee hired the folk humorist for a spot on his radio program in New York. After that, crooner Bing Crosby wanted him on his show, so he bounced back to Hollywood.

Unfortunately, Elizabeth met with an untimely death just as it looked like her husband was becoming a star. He later married Harriett Foster, who had worked as his assistant, and they added three more descendants to the Burns lineage.

With his bazooka playing and storytelling, the "Arkansas Philoso-pher" had finally made it. By 1937, Burns was a regular on the hour-long variety radio show Kraft Music Hall, starring Bing Crosby, and on other programs featuring Vallee and Charlie McCarthy. In 1941 he started his own Bob Burns Show, which played on the radio air waves until 1947.

Thanks to his increasing radio work, he began to make more films as well. His credits include *The Dawn Trail* (1931), *When a Man Rides Alone* (1933), *Big Broadcast of 1937* (1936), *Mountain Music* (1937), *The Arkansas Traveler* (1938), *I'm from Missouri* (1939), *Comin' Round the Mountain* (1940), *Belle of the Yukon* (1944), *Twilight in the Sierras* (1950).

Cleverly, Burns invested his substantial earnings in real estate in the San Fernando Valley, which boomed after World War II. He kept two hundred acres for his own use, and, after retiring from show business, he put his civil-engineering and farming-community background to work. He established a model farm facility, with its own power plant and reservoir system. Equipped with the latest machinery, the farm came to be of such interest that agricultural experts worldwide came to study Burns's accomplishments. At the time of his 1956 death, Bob Burns was one of the richest men in Hollywood.

Macdonald Carey

I n 1965, Macdonald Carey began playing Dr. Tom Horton on the
TV soap opera *Days of Our Lives*. He remained on the job for
nearly thirty years, by which time the cast had become like a family of its own. But Carey's real family often had trouble with him,
largely due to his ongoing battle with the bottle. He finally gave it up
at age sixty-nine.

It was a problem that he had inherited, and it is the major theme—
indeed the raison d'être—of his autobiography, *The Days of My Life*
(St. Martin's Press, 1991; Carey also published three volumes of poetry).
A weakness for drinking ran in the family, he tells us, and besides,
drinking during Prohibition was an extremely popular sport.

Carey managed it well, considering; he hardly wound up wandering the streets. A social animal from childhood, he achieved success in

(Photofest)

radio programs before World War II, served as a Marine, was married only once, produced six children, and had a prosperous career in theater, movies, and television.

He was born (15 March 1913) in Sioux City, Iowa, christened Edward by Elizabeth and Charles Carey, a banker. It was a close-knit, liberal, middle-class Scotch-Irish family of mostly merchants and newspapermen; Elizabeth, as a young woman, had taught violin at the Chicago Music Conservatory. She showed her youngsters how to put on shows for the family's entertainment, which Edward especially enjoyed. When he was twelve his father gave him a film projector, opening undreamed-of new horizons. He began to set his sights on show business.

Young Carey also loved music, literature, and French, and his high-school years were far from dull. With an eye on Dartmouth, he enrolled in Phillips Exeter Academy to accumulate the credits he needed to be accepted at the Ivy League school. But by 1931 the Great Depression had caught up with the Careys, who could no longer afford Dartmouth. They could still manage the University of Wisconsin, and Edward was sent there for a year before they ran out of funds for that, too. But the year had not been wasted: the young thespian got a group together and produced several plays.

During his first summer out of college, he and three friends started a singing group, entertaining between innings at Sioux City's baseball park and in speakeasies. Eventually a radio station offered them a contract. Instead, they elected to sign on as "work-a-ways"—apprentice merchant mariners, earning a penny a month—on board the steel freighter *Bessemer City,* slated to make a round-the-world voyage. One of the foursome already held his able-bodied seaman papers, and through Carey's father the other three also were able to get jobs on board the ship.

The *Bessemer City* left New York for California, by way of the Panama Canal. By the time the boys reached San Francisco, they had had enough of life at sea and left the ship. This turned out to be a fortuitous decision: the freighter sank during a fierce storm off Wales later that year.

After taking more college courses, in the summer of 1933 Carey enrolled at the University of Iowa and began acting in earnest. He studied drama under England's Stratford-on-Avon theater founder B. Iden Payne, and under E. C. Mabie, who headed the university's drama department and had previously headed Dartmouth's. Carey was cast in numerous plays, and in 1936, just before taking orals for his master of arts degree (on a straight path to a career in academia, if he wanted one), he was offered a job with the Shakespearean acting company Globe Theatre.

First playing bit parts, Carey eventually was given the role of Brutus, which resulted in leads. The group traveled all over the Midwest, performing in schools, auditoriums, tents—even, sometimes, in theaters. Carey loved the nonstop acting, realizing full well that it was invaluable experience.

Moving on to Chicago, the capital of radio at the time, he got his first big break when he was cast as the host on the popular show *First Nighter.* That led to a spot on another radio program, *Lights Out,* a forerunner of *The Twilight Zone* and *One Step Beyond.* In 1937, Macdonald Carey played the role of a young doctor in his first soap opera, NBC's *Women in White.* Next he was signed as a country doctor on his own soap, *Young Hickory.* Carey became a radio celebrity in the Windy City, appearing on numerous shows, and by late 1938 he'd decided to take on Broadway.

With his impressive previous experience, it didn't take him long to get into radio soap operas and commercials in New York. As he met agents, auditioned, and tried to get on Broadway, he took lessons in acting, singing, dancing, fencing, and judo. The twenty-five-year-old performer continued to drink too much, but he also played tennis, went to the gym, and sometimes boxed. It was through his friends and acquaintances in radio that he managed to get a three-year stint on the radio soap *Stella Dallas,* then on others, including *Young Widder Brown; Just Plain Bill; Mr. Keane, Tracer of Lost Persons;* and *Backstage Wife.*

Joining the Actors' Repertory Theatre, he appeared in a presentation of readings from several popular plays. That performance led to work in a Maplewood, New Jersey, summer theater, which, in turn, led to his being cast opposite Gertrude Lawrence in the 1941 Broadway musical *Lady in the Dark* (with Danny Kaye and Victor Mature).

By this time the twenty-six-year-old, sexually enthusiastic bachelor had met and quickly proposed to aspiring actress Betty Heckscher, the half-sister of Mrs. C. Vanderbilt Whitney. She made him wait for a few months, after which they were married in Maplewood, with Victor Mature as best man. Betty officially converted to Catholicism the same day. A week later, to satisfy her family, they were married again in an Episcopal service in Bryn Mawr, Pennsylvania—with photos that appeared in the July 1941 issue of *Town and Country* magazine. It was the beginning of a tumultuous marriage that would last for twenty-six years and produce six children.

Shortly before his marriage, while he was still playing in *Lady in the Dark*, a Paramount talent scout asked Carey to take a screen test. The studio liked what they saw, they signed him to a contract, and the Careys moved to Hollywood. After making his first two movies, *Dr. Broadway* (1942) and *Take a Letter, Darling* (1942, starring Fred MacMurray), Carey appeared in *Wake Island* (1942). This war movie so impressed the cast that many of them, including Carey himself, joined the Marine Corps after its completion.

But the Corps did not accept Carey the first time he applied—he was deemed color blind, and the fact that he was shaking uncontrollably did not help matters. Bent on becoming a Marine, he took a course (the Bates method) to correct the vision problem. This time he got in, but he was to make three more films (including Alfred Hitchcock's *Shadow of a Doubt*, 1943) before reporting to boot camp at Parris Island, resolved to defeat fascism and the Nazis.

Eight weeks of grueling boot training were spiced with the usual extra dose of unpleasant tasks assigned to anyone who might think he was special, as it was assumed all Hollywood actors did. Qualifying for Officer's Training School, Carey was sent for ten weeks to Quantico, after which he was commissioned a second lieutenant, U.S. Marine Corps Reserve. Perhaps because of his background in radio, he was next ordered to Orlando, Florida, for radar training as a fighter director, or air controller.

Ordered after Orlando to the Marine Air Station at Cherry Point, North Carolina, he was assigned to Air Warning Squadron Three (AWS 3) as ordnance officer. Betty had been able to join him by now, and they spent many hours at the officers' club mess, which was run by Vincent Sardi, of the New York restaurant. The food was excellent and the drinks cheap.

Pfc. Macdonald Carey does guard duty around his barracks, Parris Island. (Photofest)

Second Lieutenant Carey at Cherry Point, November 1943.

Drinks were plentiful at AWS 3's next stop, too: Naval Air Station, Miramar, California, where the squadron was ordered in early December 1943. The Careys lived for several months in a grand hotel, the Casa Manana, on the beach at La Jolla. At Miramar, training continued and the squadron was brought up to strength—14 officers, 258 enlisted men, and 6 Navy hospital corpsmen.

Carey's excessive drinking got him into trouble—not for the first time. Badly hung over one day when his unit was to march in a parade, he drank a half pint of bourbon to steady himself before standing in formation under a hot sun for an hour. He then staggered and careened his way through the parade, after which he was put under house arrest on the base. Finally he got to return to party central—the hotel—where, during a volleyball game, he broke his leg.

In mid-February 1944, when it came time for AWS 3 to ship out, Carey had to make a special request of his commanding officer, Capt. Harold W. Swope, to allow him to join the squadron, since he was still under house arrest. Swope allowed his return to duty, but, as a result of the parade incident, he was passed over for promotion during ensuing opportunities.

AWS 3 arrived at Espiritu Santo between 15 and 22 March 1944. While on the Pacific island, the squadron was developed into a competent, operating unit. They trained in assembling, installing, operating, and maintaining air-defense equipment; they trained with seasoned pilots, developing techniques that worked for all parties. Finally, VMTB-232 (Marine Torpedo Bomber Squadron 232) played the role of targets. Simulated attacks were planned, using "window" (a radar-jamming technique in which strips of aluminum foil dropped from raiding aircraft generated false returns on radar screens) and split raids. The exercises kept AWS 3 personnel busy: they were responsible for controlling nine day-fighter squadrons; VMF(N)-534, a Marine night-fighter squadron; and pilots in the Marine Air Group II fighter pool.

Espiritu Santo was an R and R base for American troops fighting on Guadalcanal and for the pilots who were flying combat missions along "the Slot"—New Hebrides to Bougainville. There was little to do but train and train some more. One of Carey's missions as ordnance officer was to set up perimeter defenses around recaptured or newly constructed airfields.

To keep his men proficient, he set them to work building a perimeter defense around the field at Espiritu Santo. He and his men scoured the island, stripping wrecked aircraft of their guns and retrieving anything usable from local "SeaBee" (CB, Navy Construction Battalion) junkyards. The perimeter defense line was built, and, though not impenetrable, it did provide a measure of security for the airfield.

The ever-sociable Carey befriended the torpedo bomber pilots, who sometimes took him along on their practice flights. He also was able to log some hours in Navy SNJ training aircraft. As a potential air controller, he got a good idea of what went on in the air—useful experience for an air controller.

On 23 November ASW 3 arrived at Bougainville, to await further assignment. The area was safe from enemy attack, so Carey filled his time making seashell and scrap-metal jewelry, playing poker, or sitting under a waterfall in the middle of the steamy jungle. There were also odd little adventures, such as the day when he and a friend met a Scottish couple on a nearby island who invited them to play tennis. They kept a perfectly manicured grass court, though they did not themselves play tennis, just in case someone stopped by for a visit.

Four months passed before AWS 3 participated in the invasion of Mindoro, the Philippines, on 20 March. The Japanese had already abandoned the island, and Carey and his men once again found themselves in a lull before moving forward. They did have some work to do, verifying that their radar and radio sets were in shape for the upcoming operation, but there was also a lot of poker time. They also drank, watched cockfights, and rode on transport aircraft (DC3s) to Manila. There was fighting north of the city, but in town, things were calm enough for young Marines to look around.

On 17 April 1945, the three hundred men of AWS 3, as part of the larger fleet contingent Task Group 78.2, invaded Mindanao. Again they met with no resistance: the Japanese had already retreated farther into the large island. Carey was put in charge of a platoon and ordered to proceed to Malabang airfield, held by American forces. There he was to rendezvous with the rest of his squadron, whose job it was to haul the necessary radar equipment to the field. But on the way they got lost—and came across another confused platoon, with whom they eventually located the field.

Carey spent the next seven months playing cards, collecting souvenirs, and learning chess from the natives. He continued to drink a lot, especially after the war ended and the O Club, to clear out their inventory, began giving drinks away. Carey was the last officer in the squadron to leave Mindanao. After a month's layover on Manus Island off the coast of New Guinea, he was shipped back to NAS Miramar and processed out of the Corps with an honorable discharge.

Like many postwar actors, Carey found that work was scarce, though he was fortunate in that he was still under contract and made money even when not working. But it was more than a year before he was cast in another film—*Suddenly It's Spring* (1947), starring Fred MacMurray and Paulette Goddard. In the years that followed he appeared in many more movies, including *The Great Gatsby* (1949), *South Sea Sinner* (1950, with Shelly Winters), and *John Paul Jones* (1959, with Bette Davis and Robert Stack). He kept up the partying, which did affect his work, but he pressed on regardless, serving as a board member of the Academy of Motion Picture Arts and Sciences for nine years.

In 1965 he was offered the leading role on *Days of Our Lives*. He played the chief of internal medicine at University Hospital until his death in 1994.

In 1969, after twenty-six years of an often unsettled marriage, the Careys were divorced. In January 1982, Carey's son Steve confessed to his father that he was having a problem with his drinking. That—finally—prompted Carey to turn to Alcoholics Anonymous. Carey later discovered that Steve had no drinking problem but had used the ploy to get his dad into the program. With the unflagging support of his family and longtime (since 1979) girlfriend, Lois Kraines, in 1982 Carey stopped drinking. He enjoyed twelve addiction-free years before passing away.

Barry Corbin

Texas-born and -bred Barry Corbin, television's cranky former astronaut in the series *Northern Exposure,* has had a hankering for the acting profession ever since high school. Born 16 October 1940 in Lamesa, Leonard Barrie Corbin was one of three children of Kilmer B. Corbin, a two-term Texas senator in the late 1940s and early 1950s, and his elementary-schoolteacher wife. Leonard Barrie attended Monterey High School in Lubbock, where he appeared regularly in school plays and became a member of the Future Farmers of America.

With no plans to abandon the Lone Star state, he joined the Marine Corps Reserve in March 1962 (his brother, K. B., also served in the Marine Corps Reserve). Leonard Barrie Corbin was initially attached to the 40th Rifle Company at Lubbock, and he entered recruit training as a member of the 3d Recruit Training Battalion, Marine Corps Recruit Depot, San Diego. After completing his training in June of that same year he was ordered to N Company, 2d Battalion, 2d Infantry Training Regiment, Marine Corps Base, Camp Pendleton. He stayed there until he was released from active duty in September.

Corbin remained in the Marine Corps Reserve, rejoining the 40th Rifle Company in Lubbock as an assistant Browning Automatic Rifle (BAR) man. He was discharged from the Reserves in August 1963. Corbin still maintains that although he never left California, much less saw any action, his Marine Corps training has served him well in both his public and private pursuits.

After his release from the Corps, he enrolled at Texas Tech University in Lubbock, majoring in drama. During the next several years he found acting jobs in regional theaters around the country, eventually landing a role on Broadway in 1969 in *Henry V.* Corbin continued to travel to wherever the roles were, appearing in locations such as the American Shakespeare Festival at Stratford, Connecticut; the Actor's Theatre in Louisville, Kentucky; and Pheasant Run Theatre in Chicago.

In 1972 the six-foot, solid, brown-haired and -eyed Shakespearean performer was plying his trade in Alabama, where he met fellow thespian Sue Berger. They moved together to New York City and were married in 1976. Both their family and Corbin's career began to grow, and in 1977 they relocated to California. A couple of years later he was cast in *Urban Cowboy* (1980, starring John Travolta and Debra Winger), his first movie. That major break was followed by, among many other films, *Any Which Way You Can* (1980), *Honky Tonk Man* (1982), *Wargames* (1983), *The Man Who Loved Women* (1983), *Critters II: The Main Course* (1988), *Who's Harry Crumb* (1989), and *Career Opportunities* (1991).

He has appeared in made-for-TV movies such as *Travis McGee* (1983), *Bitter Harvest* (1981), *Prime Suspect* (1982), and *The Chase* (1991). His work in miniseries includes *Lonesome Dove, Fatal Vision,* and *The Thorn Birds.* The TV series in which he's guest-starred include *Murder She Wrote, Hill Street Blues, The Magnificent Seven, Matlock, Twilight Zone, The A Team,* eight episodes of *Dallas,* and *Murphy Brown.*

On the set of CBS's *Northern Exposure,* Corbin chats with costar Rob Morrow. (Photofest)

Corbin's TV series include *The Big Easy, Raising Caine, Spies,* and *Northern Exposure.* He costarred in the latter from 1990 to 1995, which represented for him the beginning of steady, reliable work in films (rather than *Urban Cowboy,* as might have been expected). He has appeared in repertory and stock theater, on and off Broadway, and in musicals including *Oklahoma, Kiss Me Kate,* and *My Fair Lady.* The busy Corbin has also written radio plays and screenplays, and he's been featured in numerous public-service announcements as well as commercials.

Barry and Sue Corbin were divorced in 1992. He has four children and now maintains his base of operations in central Texas, where he spends as much time as possible raising Longhorn cattle and quarter horses. He also tries to make up for lost time with his daughter, whom he met only in 1991. The secret product of an early liaison, she had been adopted by a family who eventually helped her to locate her biological parents through an agency. She now helps the constantly traveling Corbin to keep things organized at the ranch, ably advised and assisted by her own two children and her three Corbin brothers.

Brian Dennehy

A big man in both frame and presence, Bridgeport, Connecticut–born (9 July 1938) Brian Marion Dennehy had no idea
what to do with himself until he discovered acting. Brian's
father, Ed, whose own father had emigrated from Ireland, was a local
reporter who read constantly and loved poetry. When he was offered
the job of editor for the Associated Press, he and wife Hannah and
their three sons (Brian was the oldest) moved across the Long Island
Sound to Brooklyn, then farther out on the island to Mineola.

Brian's Catholic parents may have been pleased about his early lean-
ing toward becoming a priest (until he discovered the carnal pleasures),
but they also knew how inquisitive he was, and, like it or not, even in
high school anyone could see how he loved acting and the theater. He
attended Mineola's Chaminade Catholic High School, where the six-
foot-three teenager went out for football. One of his teachers, an actor

(Photofest)

who was also a former football player, took note of the young athlete's strong artistic qualities. Inspired by him, Brian acted in a school production of *Macbeth*. That first theatrical experience affected him so deeply that he would feel self-realized only after he had found his way back onto the stage.

But that would take him many more years. A good student as well as a solid jock on the gridiron, Dennehy was awarded a scholarship to New York's Columbia University. Majoring in history, he also achieved honorable mention all–Ivy League as an offensive lineman for the school's team, the Lions. But after marrying in 1959, he left school without finishing his degree.

At a loss as to what to do with himself, he joined the Marine Corps on 15 September 1959. In the military, at least he would have no major career-direction decisions to make for a while.

He was ordered to the 3d Recruit Battalion, Marine Corps Depot (MCD), for training at Parris Island. After training ended in December 1959, Dennehy was assigned to A Company, 1st Battalion, 1st Infantry Training Regiment, Marine Corps Base (MCB) at Camp Lejeune, North Carolina. He completed Infantry Combat Training there in February 1960 and was next ordered to Headquarters Company, Headquarters Battalion, 2d Marine Division at Lejeune, working in the G-2 Administration Section.

In July of that year, while still at Lejeune, Dennehy changed his specialty to intelligence assistant. Almost two years later, in June 1962, he joined Headquarters Battery, 12th Marines, 3d Marine Division (Reinforced), Fleet Marine Force (FMF), which had been deployed to Okinawa since 1956. During Dennehy's one-year tour in Okinawa, support personnel were sent to South Vietnam to augment the Marine Advisory Division. Although the United States was not yet officially enmeshed in the Vietnamese conflict, there were already many U.S. military advisers in-country.

Dennehy served during a tumultuous time in Vietnam's complex, tormented history. In 1963, Buddhist monks set themselves afire in protest of the Christian-dominated government, Communists fought for control of the southern part of the country, and the future of president Ngo Dinh Diem looked increasingly dim, helped to be so by the American policy makers. Diem was overthrown on 1 November 1963, and he and his brother were murdered the next day.

Dennehy left Okinawa before the Vietnam tumult started; he was ordered back to the States in late May of 1963. He remained with the 3d Marine Division until he was detached and ordered to Depot Casual Section, Marine Corps Reserve Depot, San Diego, where he awaited release from active duty. On 5 June 1963, he was transferred to the Enlisted Volunteer Reserves, 1st Marine Corps Reserve Recruit Depot (MCRRD). On 14 September 1965, he was discharged from the inactive reserves, leaving the Marine Corps at the rank of corporal.

He returned to Long Island, where for the next several years he worked as a truck driver, bartender, salesman, and a succession of other mundane jobs, providing for his wife and his three daughters. Meanwhile, his father was pushing him to go to law school or make some other intelligent move that would result in a respectable and lucrative future. But Brian was not interested. Having served in the Marines and seen how brief life can be, he no longer entertained any notions of pursuing a serious career path that did not stimulate him.

By 1970 he had decided to go for the one job that did inspire him— acting. He began going on auditions and found parts in off-off Broadway and in local theaters around Long Island. He finally got his break in 1976, when he appeared in the play *Streamers* at Lincoln Center, New York. This led to film work in California, including in *Semi-Tough* (1977) and *F.I.S.T.* (1978). His first major movie role was that of the sheriff who drives Sylvester Stallone's Rambo to the extreme measures portrayed in *First Blood* (1982).

Since then, Brian Dennehy has become known for consistently delivering quality performances in a series of films that have brought him both critical and profitable success. The list includes *Gorky Park* (1983), *Silverado* (1985), *Cocoon* (1985), *F/X* (1986), *Best Seller* (1987), *Seven Minutes* (1989), and *Presumed Innocent* (1990). His performance in the Italian production *The Belly of an Architect* (1987) won him the best-actor award at the Chicago Film Festival.

His stage acting has featured a riveting rendition in Eugene O'Neill's four-and-a-half-hour play *The Iceman Cometh,* for which he won critical laurels. On television, his movies include *Ruby and Oswald* (1978),

Pride and Extreme Prejudice (1989), *The Lion of Africa* (1987), *Killing in a Small Town* (1990), and the taut drama *In Broad Daylight* (1991). Eloquent and outgoing, Brian Dennehy reads avidly and tries to see a lot of his daughters, two of whom followed him into the acting profession. He was divorced from their mother in 1974 and later married Jennifer Arnott, with whom he lives outside of Santa Fe, New Mexico.

(Tim Putz)

Bradford Dillman

On 14 April 1930, Bradford Dillman was the newest arrival in a prosperous, socially connected San Francisco family. Until age twelve he was groomed in the private institutions Town School for Boys and St. Ignatius High School. But when his parents, Dean and Josephine Moore Dillman, separated (and later divorced), young Brad was shipped east to Hotchkiss boarding school, in Lakeville, Connecticut.

Three thousand miles away from his parents and three siblings, the adolescent Brad sorely missed his family. The compassionate headmaster, noticing the boy's state of mind, came up with a way to shift his concentration away from the West Coast: he pushed him to get involved in school theatrical productions. Brad took to it like a tuna to the Atlantic, even though his stockbroker father, alarmed at this unpractical new interest, tried everything to dissuade him from the poverty-ridden future that surely awaited him. (Later, during yearly fishing and golfing getaways with his son and grandson, Dean would beam with fatherly pride.)

Brad had begun acting in third grade, when he was cast as a plump cherub in a Christmas pageant at the Town School. Though the diminutive devil, in his own nervousness, jostled Dillman to the floor during the production, the stunned little angel quickly bounced back. He was also an avid movie fan and, on Saturdays, he often attended three double features, all by himself. At Hotchkiss he appeared in title roles in several school plays, and at Yale University, where he started in 1947, he majored in literature and drama. During summers, he returned home to Santa Barbara and performed in summer stock.

Bradford Dillman enlisted in the U.S. Naval Reserve (V-6 program) in 1948, participating in activities during summer vacations. When he graduated from Yale, he was discharged from the V-6 program and, applying through the university's NROTC administration unit, he enlisted in the Marine Corps as an officer candidate. (His older brother, Dean, had gone through Marine boot camp in San Diego, served in a communications company, and been discharged as a private first class.)

Private Dillman was ordered to Parris Island for officer-candidate training and was commissioned a second lieutenant, Marine Corps Reserve, in September 1951. In early 1952, by which time he was platoon leader of a rifle company, Dillman was making ready to sail from San Diego for Korea as part of the 23d Replacement Draft. A few days before his unit was to leave, he was called to the main base, where a personnel officer changed his orders.

"Dillman," he recalled the personnel officer saying, "do you realize you're the only one of 55,000 Marines currently on this post who's had any experience as an actor?"

"So?"

"So we're pulling you off the boat. We're making you an instructor. You will teach combat veterans how to teach what they've learned in an illuminating and interesting manner."

Dillman was reassigned as an instructor, ordered to teach in the Instructors' Orientation Course. He was sent to Camp Del Mar, located across from Camp Pendleton on Highway 101, California. Two other officer-teachers handled organizing the course; Dillman's

In an Instructors' Orientation Course at Camp Del Mar, 1st Lt.
Bradford Dillman's students were combat veterans. (Bradford
Dillman collection)

job, as the actor, was to present it. He taught communication techniques and podium tricks to classes of about fifty, using numerous off-color jokes for the all-important entertainment ingredient of education. And, since many of the students wrote to Dillman over the years, his acting background must, indeed, have served him well.

He was discharged in 1953 as a first lieutenant. His military service completed, Dillman aimed his energies at getting onto Broadway. With former Yale classmate and future novelist John Knowles, he shared a tiny one-bedroom apartment in New York's Hell's Kitchen, traditionally a popular thespian neighborhood for its proximity to the theater district. He found some work off Broadway and on live television, but steady employment as an actor did not come readily. Dillman supplemented his income with various jobs, including lobster-shift proofreading on Wall Street and desk-clerking at a hotel.

A major part of his job at this prostitution-friendly establishment was to recognize the women who brought in the johns, because these were the prostitutes who were in the employ of the mobsters who ran the racket, in a complicated deal that included paying off certain cops. Women who worked independently of the mob were fair game and were not supposed to be allowed into the hotel. But one night Dillman made a mistake. Thinking he recognized a very young woman, he was about to let her and her client into a room when the police barreled onto the scene, arrested the girl, and fined the hotel's mobster owner. That was the end of that source of income—but, fortunately, not of Brad Dillman.

The brown-haired, brown-eyed, lanky actor's career began to take an upturn when he was accepted into the Actor's Studio, where he worked under the tutelage of Lee Strasberg (at the same time as did Marilyn Monroe). His big break came in 1955, when he was cast as a soldier in the off-Broadway production *Third Person*. That performance attracted the notice of director José Quintero, who asked him to audition for Eugene O'Neill's *Long Day's Journey into Night*. After final approval from the playwright's widow, former actress Carlotta Monterey O'Neill, Bradford Dillman was cast as the character based on the young Eugene O'Neill. The 1956 production was a much heralded success, for which Dillman received critical plaudits.

The play went to London in 1957, and a year later Dillman left the company to begin his movie career. He signed with Twentieth Century-

Fox. After appearing in a few nondescript movies, he gave a star-quality performance as the killer in *Compulsion* (1959), a movie version of the notorious 1924 Loeb-Leopold murder case. He and costars Orson Welles and Dean Stockwell shared a best-actor award at the 1959 Cannes International Film Festival for their superb work in the film.

Needless to say, more work followed, including *In Love and War* (1958, in which he played a Marine), *Crack in the Mirror* (1960), *Francis of Assisi* (1961), *Suppose They Gave a War and Nobody Came* (1970), *Escape from the Planet of the Apes* (1971), *The Iceman Cometh* (1973), *The Enforcer* (1976), *Piranha* (1978), *The Swarm* (1978), and *Guyana, Cult of the Damned* (1980).

Known as an independent who's dared to be happy, when Dillman married Cecelia "Suzy" Parker (in 1963; his second marriage), both made the uncommon choice to focus on raising a close family. A former actress and fashion model, Parker devoted herself to holding down the fort at home, while Dillman concentrated on getting as much work as he could to bring in the bacon and get the six kids regular checkups and off to good schools. He made a conscious choice, as he put it in his memoir, *Are You Anybody?* (Fithian, 1997), in favor of "the Safeway Solution."

That solution did not keep the witty, congenial Dillman from winning universal respect in his field. He has performed onstage and in nearly countless television shows, including the *Hallmark Hall of Fame, Kraft Television Theatre, Omnibus, The FBI, Mission Impossible, Ironside, Barnaby Jones, Falcon Crest,* and *Hotel.* He showed up eight times in television's *Murder, She Wrote,* more often than any other guest star. In addition to his Cannes Film Festival acting award, he won a Golden Globe award in 1958 for most promising new star, and an Emmy in 1975 for his performance in *The Last Bride of Salem,* produced by the *Afternoon Playbreak.* He was nominated for another Emmy for *The Voice of Charlie Pont.*

Dillman was married once before (1956–60) to aspiring actress Frieda Harding, the mother of his first two children. Aside from his family, he loves pro football and writing, interests that he pursues from his Santa Barbara home. In addition to his memoir, he's also published *Inside the New York Giants* (Third Story Books, 1994) and *Dropkick: A Football Fantasy* (Cronopio, 1998).

Camp Joseph H. Pendleton

In the eighteenth century, Spanish Franciscans founded missions along the California coast from San Diego to San Francisco, in their quest to "civilize" the Indians. After Mexico won its independence from Spain in 1822, the missionaries unsuccessfully lobbied the Mexican government to hold mission lands in trust for the Indians until they had been deemed sufficiently enlightened to handle the management of such a weighty responsibility.

In 1833, Upper California governor Jose Figueroa officially gave the Indians half of the lands, but unofficially his decree was never put into effect. The lands were given, instead, to military men and those who had been politically helpful to the Mexican government.

On the 226,000-acre Rancho Santa Margarita y Las Flores had been the San Luis Rey mission, founded in 1798. Before the Marines bought the ranch in 1942, most of their activities in the region had centered around the base at San Diego. But when the Training Center at Camp Elliott was activated in April 1942, continued expansion and increased concentration of Marine Corps activities on the West Coast necessitated yet more land for training purposes.

On 10 March 1942, the U.S. Navy Department announced the purchase of approximately 132,000 acres of the Rancho Santa Margarita y Las Flores. Construction of the base began on 23 March 1942, starting with training facilities for amphibious forces. The new base was named after Maj. Gen. Joseph H. Pendleton, who had started Marine Corps activities in the San Diego area in 1914, when his 4th Regiment had established the first Marine barracks there. By September 1942, Camp Pendleton at Oceanside was ready for its first troops. The 9th Marines, who were at Camp Elliott, were ordered to the new base, arriving on 4 September 1942. President Franklin Delano Roosevelt dedicated Camp Pendleton on 25 September, suggesting that the "romantic flavor of this old Mexican land grant . . . be preserved."

Accordingly, the California Historical Society oversaw restorations of the ranch house, bunkhouse, winery, and gardens. For furniture, benefactors donated antiques. The oldest building, the winery, was to be redesigned as a chapel, along the lines of an old mission chapel. All went well until January 1943, when massive storms destroyed most of the landscaping and blew trees into the buildings. The winery roof was torn, crushing some of the roof tile. Tile was broken as well in the bunkhouse, and a ranch-house chimney was blown over, flooding the house.

In June 1944, the Training Command, Fleet Marine Force, took over instruction in all branches of the service at Camp Pendleton. The training for infantry-men was probably the most nerve-racking; certainly it conveyed a sense of the realities of war. Various weapons, both U.S. and enemy, including rockets, flares, flamethrowers, rifles, and machine guns, were fired over the troops' heads to familiarize them with the sounds of battle. Loudspeakers added still more noises to the chaotic environment. At the Infiltration Range, troops crawled over 150 yards of rough terrain that was littered with obstacles.

Other courses given at Pendleton included the Combat Conditioning Course and the Amphibious Training Course. Both Raiders and Seabees went through the curriculum, which featured abandon-ship jumps, landing-boat exercises, com-bat swimming, judo, and fighting with knives and bayonets. On Camp Pendle-ton's beaches, the Marine Corps offered what may have been the best training for amphibious fighting in the world. In 1944, as part of the Lend-Lease Act, twenty to forty-five Netherlands Marines were instructed each month. Courses they took included communications, infantry weapons, combat conditioning, motor transport, tank and antitank, and amphibian tractors.

By September 1944, many of the Marine Corps units fighting in the Pacific had been trained at Pendleton. Comdt. Lt. Gen. A. A. Vandegrift requested that Camp Pendleton be designated a permanent Marine Corps establishment. Post-war needs should be taken into consideration, he maintained: the Corps needed a permanent Pacific amphibious training base, an area in which all types of train-ing could be conducted. Pendleton not only fulfilled all the requirements, but also offered a superior boat basin, as well as the many facilities that had been built there. On 14 October 1944 the request was approved.

Since the end of World War II, Camp Pendleton, with its seventeen miles of prime Southern California coastline, has continued to develop and expand its training facilities and activities. It has met the demands of both the Korean and Vietnam Wars, as well as those of continually evolving global military missions.

The home of the I Marine Expeditionary Force (MEF), 1st Marine Divison, and 1st Force Service Support Group (FSSG), the base continues to be the most active training facility among the military services. Some thirty-five thousand Marine and Navy men and women, along with their families, are today residents of Camp Pendleton. The area has often been used as a site for shooting scenes of the many movies on which the Corps has provided assistance to directors and producers.

Gene Hackman

Hardworking, down-to-earth Gene Hackman, who has so often captivated audiences with his portrayals of "the good, the bad, and the funny" (*Washington Post*, 6 October 1996, G6), plays every role as if it were the most important of his very impressive career. Sometimes described as average looking, this tall, intense man with the leathered face, exposed forehead, and astute blue-gray gaze conveys solidity and uniqueness.

To explain his apparent toughness, he is often characterized as a former Marine. But Hackman has said that his early acting days in New York, struggling with odd jobs to make the rent, toughened him up at least as much. It was the Corps that inculcated him with a sense of discipline, though, which has served him well throughout the years in his difficult chosen profession.

Eugene Alden Hackman was born in San Bernardino, California,

(Photofest)

on 30 January 1931. He was raised in Danville, Illinois, where his father, Eugene Ezra Hackman, was a pressman for the Danville *Commercial News*. His grandfather had also worked there for many years as a reporter. His college-educated mother enjoyed playing music, but Eugene Ezra apparently was not sufficiently entertained: he took off when Gene was thirteen years old, leaving his wife to finish raising Gene and his younger brother by herself.

High school was difficult for the embarrassed actor-in-the-making, enraged at having been abandoned—an unusual and very noticeable situation in rural Danville. He could not bring himself even to ask a girl out on a date, and was anxious to get away from the family responsiblities that he felt his father had thrown entirely onto his youthful shoulders. (He later looked for and located his father, with whom he reconciled even though Eugene Ezra would not discuss the split-up.) Gene played on the basketball team and spent as much time as he could in movie theaters, imagining himself in the shoes of Errol Flynn or James Cagney.

Finally he just had to get out there and see what was happening in the rest of the world. His mother disagreed, but he left anyway and informed a Marine Corps recruiter that he was one year older than he actually was. Hackman joined the Corps on 13 February 1947; he had turned sixteen one month earlier. He was shipped off to boot camp at Parris Island.

Surviving that experience, he was assigned to the Signal Battalion, Marine Training and Replacement Command, Camp Pendleton, and was later ordered to Headquarters and Service Battalion, 2d Marine Division, Camp Lejeune. He was next sent to Treasure Island, San Francisco, and shipped out on the USS *General Randall* (AP-115) for Pearl Harbor. From there Hackman was flown via government air to Tsingtao, China.

In the fall of 1945, just after the end of World War II, some 53,000 Marines had been sent to North China, tasked with disarming and replacing the Japanese garrisons in communications centers and ports. They also repatriated Japanese military personnel and civilians and kept as many leftover weapons as possible away from the Communists, who, with 170,000 regular troops in the area, were poised to take over.

U.S. Marines were caught in a lose-lose political situation, in which the United States backed the corrupt Chiang Kai-shek and his poorly led Nationalist forces against the better-intentioned but Communist Mao Tse-tung. Marines held back Communist advances in critical parts of the country, bolstering the Nationalists while charged at the same time with remaining neutral.

They protected lines of communication, guarded supply and ammunition storage areas, removed road blocks, and held the dedicated, aggressive Chinese Communists in check for as long as they could. Strangely, the Marines were assisted by Japanese prisoners of war, who guarded their erstwhile massive supply depots and protected bridges, railroad tracks, and roads. To perform these duties and protect themselves, the Japanese prisoners were allowed to keep one rifle and five rounds of ammunition for every ten men.

By the time Pfc. Gene Hackman disembarked from a U.S. transport plane at Tsingtao on 16 April 1948, the American Marine presence in China was increasingly threatened as the Communists steadily gained strength. Attached to Headquarters and Service Battalion, 3d Marine Division, Fleet Marine Force, Pacific, Hackman spent almost a year in China, performing guard duties and working as a telephone lineman and radio announcer.

By 3 February 1949, any Marines who were still in Tsingtao were aboard ships, Gene Hackman included. By the time he sailed, on 17 March aboard the USS *Chilton* (AP-38), the Communists had all but won total control of the country. All remaining Marines would leave China by 26 May.

Hackman disembarked in San Diego on 1 June 1949, and on 26 August he was attached to the Headquarters Company, 1st Marine Division. That fall, the athletically inclined eighteen-year-old played with the unit's football squad and was on the track and swimming teams. He was honorably discharged from the Marine Corps at Marine Barracks, Great Lakes Naval Training Center, on 12 February 1950.

But his military days were not over yet. The next day he re-upped, remaining in the service for another four years. He served with the 2d Marine Division at Camp Lejeune. Gene Hackman finally left the Corps as a private first class in February 1954, after seven years in the

On 11 October 1945, banners across the streets of Tsingtao proclaimed the arrival of Maj. Gen. Lemuel C. Shepherd, Jr.'s, Sixth Marine Division. By the time Hackman arrived in 1948, Mao's forces were steadily gaining strength and U.S. presence was winding down.

Corps. He was entitled to wear the China Service Medal and the Good Conduct Medal.

Hackman had earned his high-school equivalency diploma while in the service, and now, with an interest in journalism, he began taking courses at the University of Illinois. But that didn't click, and after several months, he quit and thumbed his way to New York. Using his GI Bill entitlement, Hackman next attended the School of Radio Technique, acquiring skills that he subsequently put to good use in jobs in Florida and Illinois. Radio work didn't cut it either, in the final analysis, so he went back to New York and tried commercial art courses at the Art Student League.

In the end, Gene Hackman relocated to California to study acting, which he'd wanted to do ever since childhood. At the Pasadena Playhouse he met and befriended Dustin Hoffman, who, like himself, was not thought to be a likely star candidate. The two later shared an apartment in New York while they pursued their shared quest of trying to become successful actors, which took many years for both.

Hackman returned to New York in 1956. He sold shoes, drove a truck, and worked as a doorman between going on auditions. He found various roles off Broadway and on live television, gradually and painstakingly working his way up to meatier roles on Broadway (starting in 1964 with *Any Wednesday*). In 1961 he got his first movie work, playing a policeman in *Mad Dog Coll*. Three years later he appeared in *Lilith* (1964, starring Warren Beatty, who later recommended him for 1967's *Bonnie and Clyde*). In 1963 he won the Clarence Derwent Award for actor with the most potential for his performance in Irwin Shaw's *Children from Their Games*.

When Gene Hackman met Marlon Brando in 1965, he was expecting to find himself in the presence of some sort of deity. The fact that Brando was instead quite human and approachable, much like himself, convinced Hackman that he too might be able to make it big, someday. But for most of the 1960s he was too busy to worry about it, as he appeared in TV programs including the *U.S. Steel Hour, Defenders, Route 66, The FBI,* and *Invaders*. A series of films followed, and by 1967 Gene Hackman was nominated for an Oscar for best supporting actor for his brilliant rendition of Clyde's yokel brother, Buck Barrow, in *Bonnie and Clyde.*

He was nominated a second time for *I Never Sang for My Father* (1970), and a year later, his portrayal of the hard-boiled, rule-breaking narcotics cop Popeye Doyle in *The French Connection* (1971) won him a Best Actor Oscar. Working almost nonstop since then, Hackman has appeared in three Superman movies as the supremely evil and witty Lex Luthor. His numerous other films include *Young Frankenstein* (1974; a cameo performance), *The Conversation* (1974), *Hoosiers* (1986), *No Way Out* (1987), *Mississippi Burning* (1988; his powerful performance earned him another Oscar nomination), and *The Firm* (1993). He was awarded a second Oscar for his best-supporting performance in *Unforgiven* (1992).

Married twice—to Fay Maltese, the mother of his three children, from 1956 to 1986; now to musician Betsy Arakawa—Hackman settled several years ago in Santa Fe. For fun he used to like flying planes or racing cars, but these days he has calmed down and prefers making art (painting, drawing, sculpting), listening to his wife play the piano, and going to the opera. And, fortunately for his appreciative audience, one of the things Gene Hackman still seems to like best is working at his chosen profession.

George Roy Hill

Before he became the independently minded and disciplined, extremely creative, and prolific director who's been known to walk off the set while suggesting to producers that they have sex with themselves, George Roy Hill had several other jobs. He was a jazz singer in France, a reporter in Texas, an actor on both sides of the Atlantic, and an aviator in the Marines.

He was born in Minneapolis on 20 December 1922, into a family of midwestern businessmen and journalists of Irish descent. By the time he was nine, his parents, George R. and Helen Frances (Owens) Hill, allowed the youngster to indulge his passion for aviation at nearby Cedar Airport, where he spent many after-school hours. He knew all about stunt fliers like Frank Clarke and Roy Wilson; he could tell you that Jimmy Doolittle was the first pilot who successfully did

(Photofest)

an outside loop; he could rattle off the records of Eddie Rickenbacker, Ernst Udet, and other World War I aces, with particular emphasis on Speed Holman, who flew past grandstands at state fairs upside down —and was killed in Omaha while doing so.

During the 1920s, World War I flying aces gleefully "barnstormed" around the country in Jenny biplanes, landing in fields next to county and state fairs. There they put on air shows, and a dollar would buy you an open-cockpit airplane ride. But as commercial aviation steadily grew during the 1930s, the old barnstormers found themselves all but out of business. Hill, enthralled by their acrobatics and the freedom of the skies, started flying at age sixteen.

The lively lad was sent to Blake prep school in Hopkins, Minnesota, after which it was on to Yale. There he pursued his other great loves, history and music. He headed the Yale dramatic club, sang in the glee club, and performed in many song-and-dance productions.

Earning his bachelor's degree in 1943, he joined the Marines. They taught him how to really fly, then sent him to the South Pacific. There, toward the end of World War II, George Roy Hill piloted transport planes. It was not as illustrious as the duty his World War I heroes had served, but still, he was a Marine Corps pilot, serving his country in wartime. Like many other transport pilots, Hill logged hundreds of hours over endless Pacific waters, flying cargo, mail, passengers, air-craft parts. . . .

Though it may have seemed like routine duty to the pilots, their role in keeping lifelines open was crucial to those engaged in combat. As they landed in barren island fields, pilots and their crews welcomed a cold beer, a small reprieve that alone could offset the heat and humidity.

After the war, Hill moved briefly to Texas and worked as a reporter for a newspaper. Then, putting his GI Bill entitlement to good use, he went to Dublin, Ireland, to attend Trinity College, where he studied James Joyce's use of musical forms in *Ulysses* and *Finnegans Wake,* receiving the bachelor of letters in 1949. He then joined Cyril Cusack's repertory company and toured as an actor with the famous Abbey Players before returning to the States.

Accepted into Margaret Webster's Shakespeare Repertory Com-pany, he continued to act and tour. In 1951 he married the company's star, actress Louisa Horton, with whom he went on to produce four children. Looking for greater security and stability, Hill eventually accepted a steady job in the radio soap opera *John's Other Wife*.

But his job security was short lived. During the Korean War, the Marines called Hill back. In 1951, he reported for jet-fighter training at Marine Corps Air Station (MCAS), Cherry Point, North Carolina. He served there for eighteen months flying F9F Panther jets, and eventually he reached the rank of captain.

One night he flew into Atlanta, Georgia, in a thick fog. A ground controller had to talk him down, a terrifying experience that he had no desire to repeat. But it gave him an idea for a script about fliers in Korea, *My Brother's Keeper*. He wrote it, and the Kraft TV Theater bought it. Starring Rod Steiger, with Hill as another member of the cast, the show aired in 1953 to great reviews. It won Kraft's Best TV Play award and a job for Hill with the Kraft Theater—and his photo in *Time* magazine.

Hill flew Panther jets like these F9F-5s, training here at MCAS Kaneohe Bay, Oahu, with the 1st Provisional Marine Air-Ground Task Force.

At Kraft, Hill worked first as a story editor, then assistant director, and finally director. In the latter capacity, he scored major hits such as *A Night to Remember* (1954, about the *Titanic*; it won him an Emmy for writing it and another for directing it), *The Helen Morgan Story* (1954), and *Judgment at Nuremberg* (1957).

Moving on to Broadway, he directed the Pulitzer Prize– and New York Drama Critics Circle Award–winning *Look Homeward, Angel* (1957–59), based on Thomas Wolfe's novel, starring Hugh Griffith as Wolfe's father; *The Gang's All Here; Greenwillow; Moon in a Rainbow Shawl;* and Tennessee Williams's *Period of Adjustment* (1960).

It was Williams's play that led him to movie land. Hill made his debut by directing the film version (1962), which was also Jane Fonda's debut in a major role. Then came Lillian Hellman's *Toys in the Attic* (1963), *The World of Henry Orient* (1964, starring Peter Sellers), *Hawaii* (1966), *Thoroughly Modern Millie* (1967), and *Butch Cassidy and the Sundance Kid* (1969).

Butch opened in New Haven, Connecticut, because Hill had offered to donate all proceeds from the premiere to Yale for a filmmaking course. He also gave the Yale Art School all proceeds from the documentary of *Butch*'s making, *The Making of Butch Cassidy and the Sundance Kid* (1970), filmed at the same time as the movie. The documentary (which was Hill's own idea) has since been shown on TV and in museums, including New York's Museum of Modern Art.

Butch also won George Roy Hill an Academy Award nomination for best director. A few years later he did win the Oscar, for *The Sting* (1973). The Cannes Film Festival also honored him, with the Jury Prize for *Slaughterhouse Five* (1972).

The Great Waldo Pepper (1975) followed these acclaimed efforts, which Hill also wrote and produced. During the filming, for the sake of authenticity, he insisted that most of the scenes—except one that might have really killed Susan Sarandon—be shot in the air. Thus, Robert Redford walked on an airplane wing three thousand feet above ground, as studio personnel watched in dread.

After *Waldo,* in 1975 Universal Studios signed the multitalented director to a nearly unheard-of agreement: complete autonomy for his company, Pan Arts, for five years, to produce fifteen projects: movies, TV, stage plays, whatever Hill wanted, providing he directed three of them himself. Hill's many renowned endeavors since then have included *Slap Shot* (1977), *The World According to Garp* (1982, which he also produced), *The Little Drummer Girl* (1984), and *Funny Farm* (1988).

For many years, Hill commuted between his family's New York brownstone and his Los Angeles pied-à-terre, flying his twin-engine Comanche. But he stopped that as air traffic around the major airports became increasingly dense and perilous. For fun, he still flew his 1939 Waco UPF-7 biplane.

Called shy by some reporters, George Roy Hill has eschewed interviews and talk shows, preferring his privacy. Dressed comfortably in time-tested apparel, he has preferred telling self-deprecatory jokes and anecdotes as he tipples whiskey with friends in a bar at the end of a shooting day, leaving the public to view his movies, rather than his person. Lanky and fun-loving, the blue-eyed Irish American has concentrated on playing his one hour of Bach each morning on the piano, then on making the best movie he possibly can.

Harvey Keitel

This Brooklyn-born, streetwise actor had to keep after his chosen occupation for a long time before his became a well-known name. The youngest of three children of an Orthodox Jewish couple who had emigrated from Poland (his father) and Romania (his mother), Keitel was born on 13 May 1939 in Brighton Beach. Both parents worked hard to provide for their brood, his father sewing in a garment factory, his mother waiting tables.

Keitel's playground was Coney Island and the Atlantic Ocean, where he fished and swam and watched the weekly fireworks. Sometimes he sold confetti and used the earnings to buy a hotdog or go on one of the amusement-park rides. During the school year he didn't study much but managed to do well anyway, thanks in large part to the efforts of his grandfather.

(Photofest)

Even with that help, at Abraham Lincoln and then Alexander Hamilton high schools, he lost interest completely. When he wasn't hanging around the candy store, he might be found playing pool, doing his best to emulate his heroes James Dean, Marlon Brando, and John Cassavetes. He tried vocational school but tired of that too, and the regular high school wouldn't take him back. Searching for adventure, he finally enlisted in the Marine Corps. It was 1956, and Keitel was seventeen years old.

He was sent to Parris Island boot camp, and "when I got off that train," he said in a June 1996 *Leatherneck* magazine interview, "I felt like I was in hell." But he adjusted, and during night-combat training at Camp Geiger, North Carolina, his instructor taught him something that changed his life. "You couldn't see a thing," he told *Leatherneck*. "After awhile you could just make out the silhouette of the instructor. He said, 'You're all afraid of the dark. We're all afraid of what we don't know, and you don't know the darkness. I am going to teach you to live in the dark so you will no longer be afraid of it.' That fear of the unknown is normal and that it can be overcome by learning about it was a basic philosophical concept that has stayed with me ever since."

After infantry training, Keitel was ordered to the 2d Battalion, 8th Marines, 2d Marine Division, assigned to Company G. He wanted to go to Ranger School and had already begun the rigorous testing to compete for acceptance when he discovered that he didn't have enough time left in his enlistment to qualify. He agreed to extend his time if he could be guaranteed parachute school, but that proved to be impossible. Ranger School was out—but not travels afar.

Trouble in the Middle East called for a U.S. presence in Lebanon, and in July 1958, Harvey Keitel, with the 2d Battalion, 8th Marines, flew into Beirut. They were taken out to ships and then landed from there, with the assignment of cargo handling and serving as the shore party. They stayed for three months, but Keitel volunteered to stay on with the 3d Battalion, 6th Marines, "dug in on a mountain top overlooking Beirut," he said in *Leatherneck*.

In Beirut, unsurprisingly, Keitel had to deal with anti-Semitism, something he'd occasionally encountered in the Corps. But he was always able to hold his own, and he still treasures the sense of self-respect that he learned in the Marines.

Marines on Beirut patrol, 1958.

The Marines left Lebanon after elections had been held, and Keitel was back at Lejeune by Christmas. He was assigned, for the remainder of his time, to the 6th Marines's regimental gym, where he worked on his wrestling skills. On 17 July 1959, he was discharged.

It was in the Corps that Keitel began to take an interest in reading, for the first time in his life. Inspired by his instructors and commanding officers, he earned his high-school-equivalency diploma and took college courses while in the service.

Back in New York, Keitel took courses in stenography while working odd jobs, after which he began what would turn out to be an eight-year stint as a court stenographer at the Manhattan Criminal Court. While holding down this position, he became interested in the drama classes that a fellow stenographer mentioned, and he began taking nighttime classes.

He liked them so much that he moved to Greenwich Village and focused on developing his new skill, while going to court for his day job. In the early sixties he began appearing in plays, including off Broadway in *Up to Thursday*, written by Sam Shepard. That was the same year (1965) that he responded to a call for actors placed by New York University filmmaking student Martin Scorsese.

It was not the beginning of a catapult to stardom. But Keitel's leading role in Scorsese's first effort, *Who's That Knocking at My Door?* (1968) did attract the notice of a *New York Times* reviewer, and it was the beginning of a lasting and fruitful association between the budding actor and the budding director.

Keitel continued to work in theater and summer stock, paying the bills with his court job and developing his craft under the influence of Lee Strasberg and Stella Adler. In 1970 he worked with Scorsese again, this time appearing in the documentary *Street Scenes*. He then played the lead in Scorsese's first big picture, *Mean Streets* (1973), opposite future close friend Robert De Niro. Both actors and the director won rave reviews, but for Keitel, unlike for the other two, *Mean Streets* somehow failed to lead to stardom.

Keitel continued to plug away nevertheless, taking classes at the Actor's Studio and working in off-off and off-Broadway productions. Then lucrative work at the court went to another stenographer when Keitel agreed to play the lead in Scorsese's next effort, *Alice Doesn't Live Here Any More* (1975). This time, his terrifying, thoroughly believable rendition of a violent lover led to more work on screen and stage, including playing opposite former Marine George C. Scott in Arthur Miller's *Death of a Salesman*. He rejoined friends Scorsese and De Niro in *Taxi Driver* (1976) and costarred with Keith Carradine in director Ridley Scott's first major film, *The Duellists* (1977).

Although Keitel worked fairly steadily thereafter, it took several more movies, including *Welcome to L.A.* (1976), *Blue Collar* (1978), *The Border* (1981), *Wise Guys* (1986), and *The Last Temptation of Christ* (1988), before he at last joined the major leagues. Critics applauded his interpretation of gangster Mickey Cohen in Barry Levinson's *Bugsy* (1991); they hailed him as well for his work in *Mortal Thoughts* (1991), *Thelma and Louise* (1991), and *Sister Act* (1992). It was mostly his role in *Bugsy* that earned him, among other important tributes, the National Society of Film Critics' vote for best supporting actor of 1991, as well as an Academy Award nomination.

Harvey Keitel has gone on to appear in numerous other acclaimed films, including Quentin Tarantino's *Reservoir Dogs* (1992); Abel Ferrara's *Bad Lieutenant* (1992); Jane Campion's *The Piano* (1993), which shared the Palme d'Or at the Cannes Film Festival; and Tarantino's *Pulp Fiction* (1994), also a Palme d'Or winner.

Still based mostly in New York City (in a TriBeCa loft), the high-strung, generous, tenacious, extremely talented, and—finally—in-demand Harvey Keitel maintains another residence in California. He helps out with fund-raising efforts for school wrestling programs, and he still reads voraciously. He and actress Lorraine Bracco parted ways in 1991. He spends as much time as he can with their daughter, Stella, encouraging her to read a lot.

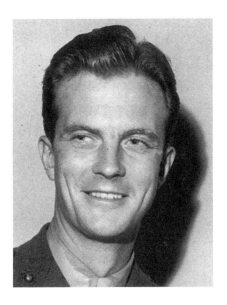

Bill Lundigan

Irish-Catholic-issued Bill Lundigan was born in Syracuse, New York (12 June 1914), to Martha and Michael Lundigan, whose name was originally O'Lundrigan. Bill was the oldest of four sons. His father owned a shoe store located in the same building as CBS affiliate radio station WFBL, and Bill spent many free hours in the station's offices, enthralled. He picked up know-how from watching radio productions, and by age ten he was playing roles in children's shows.

By age sixteen he was producing shows of his own. One of his masters of ceremony was eleven-year-old Gordon MacRae, who would later star in the musicals *Oklahoma* (1955) and *Carousel* (1956). After Syracuse high school, the young entrepreneur, imbued with a strong sense of family ties and reponsibilities as well as the value of a good education, went on to major in law during his two years at Syracuse University.

(Photofest)

But while he was still hitting the law books, an opportunity opened up at WFBL: Bill Lundigan became a radio announcer. This was far more stimulating than the future prospect of becoming a lawyer, and he eventually became the station's production manager. With a solid career in radio already mapped out and well under way, Lundigan met Universal Studios production chief Charles Rogers when he visited Syracuse.

Rogers was intrigued by the Irishman's radio-quality voice, good looks, and natural charm. He arranged for a screen test and, in 1937, Lundigan signed a contract with Universal and was off to Hollywood. Before long, his parents also relocated there.

For the next six years, the handsome bachelor played the blue-eyed, six-foot-plus-tall juvenile in numerous B quality movies for Universal, Warner Brothers (with whom he signed in 1939), and MGM. His credits include *The Old Maid* (1939, with Bette Davis), *Three Smart Girls Grow Up* (1939, with Deanna Durbin), *Santa Fe Trail* (1940), *The Case of the Black Parrot* (1941, in which he played the lead), and *The Shot in the Dark* (1941, also a lead role). In the last film he made before joining the military, Lundigan teamed up with Wallace Beery in *Salute to the Marines* (1943).

By then the United States was involved in World War II, and Lundigan, instilled with a strong sense of patriotic allegiance, joined the Marine Corps on 26 May 1943. After completing boot camp, he trained at the Marine base at Quantico as a combat photographer. While there, the young man-about-town met Washington, D.C., native Rena Morgan. They corresponded throughout his wartime service, and in 1945 they were married (and remained so for the rest of Lundigan's life, producing a daughter).

On 5 August 1944, Cpl. Bill Lundigan flew to San Francisco and then Pearl Harbor. Catching a flight to Pavuvu Island in the Russell Island Group and arriving on 13 August, he embarked on the USS *Du Page* (APA-41) on 26 August. He arrived in Guadalcanal the next day and participated in amphibious landing operations and training.

Less than a month later, on 15 September, as a member of the 3d Battalion, 1st Marines, 1st Marine Division, Lundigan took part in the invasion of Peleliu island, in the Palau group. His assignment was to film the battle.

Lundigan *(fourth from right, pipe in mouth)* and the photographers of the 1st Marine Division, Peleliu, September 1944.

On Wana Ridge, Okinawa, infantrymen of the 1st Marine Division fire at Japanese installations in the fight for Shuri Castle, 21 May 1945.

Most historians now agree that the invasion of Peleliu, five hundred miles east of the Philippines, was not necessary. Adm. Bull Halsey, commander of the Western Pacific Task Forces, opposed it, fearing another bloodbath like Tarawa. That assessment turned out to be accurate: for the Marines, the battle for Peleliu was one of the bloodiest encounters of the war. Casualties were staggering on both sides, with 1,124 Marines killed, 5,024 wounded, and 117 missing. The Army counted 277 soldiers killed and 1,008 wounded. The Japanese lost 10,200, with 302 taken prisoner.

After the island had been secured, Lundigan's unit returned to Guadalcanal for additional training. Next he embarked aboard the USS *Burleigh* (APA-95), bound for Okinawa. On 1 April 1945, he became part of the invasion force as a combat photographer, documenting for posterity and for military analysis one of the most costly battles of the war for both sides, a battle that all too many of his comrades would not survive.

Lundigan no doubt considered that he had already been through some ferocious experiences at Peleliu—but Okinawa was even worse. It took eighty-two days to secure the island, at a cost of 75,000 American casualties (548,000 servicemen had participated) from units of all the services, ashore and afloat.

Much of the battle-action footage that Lundigan shot on Peleliu and Okinawa appeared in wartime film documentaries, including the twenty-minute *Fury in the Pacific* (1945). It is likely that he also narrated the award-winning film shot by Louis Hayward and his photographic team, *With the Marines at Tarawa* (1944).

Surviving Okinawa, he was returned to the U.S. Naval Hospital, San Diego, for treatment of a spinal condition. Bill Lundigan was honorably discharged from the Corps as a corporal on 5 October 1945, entitled to wear the Presidential Unit Citation, the Asiatic-Pacific Area Campaign Medal with two bronze stars, and the World War II Victory Medal.

Returning to Hollywood to resume his career, he found, as did most actors returning from the war, that roles were harder to come by. A new constellation of stars, including Peter Lawford, Gregory Peck, Walter Pidgeon, John Wayne, and Van Johnson, now lit up the marquees, and it was they who were getting most of the steady work.

Blasting caves in Japanese-held hills, Peleliu, September 1944.

Lundigan was cast in two movies released in 1947, *Dishonored Lady* and *The Fabulous Dorseys.*

Two years later he appeared in *Follow Me Quietly* and *Pinky,* and from then on, known as a level-headed, considerate, dedicated actor sans world-owes-me attitude, the would-have-been lawyer and erstwhile radio career man worked steadily in either movies or television opposite actresses such as Dorothy McGuire, Jeanne Crain, June Haver, and Marilyn Monroe (in *Love Nest,* 1951).

He starred in a few films, notably *I'd Climb the Highest Mountain* (1951). Other movies in which he was cast, usually as the blandish nice guy, include *The Underwater City* (1962), *The Way West* (1967, costarring Kirk Douglas, Robert Mitchum, Richard Widmark, and Lola Albright), and *Where Angels Go, Trouble Follows* (1968).

On television, Lundigan hosted the series *Climax* (1954–58) and *Shower of Stars* (1956–57). He frequently appeared in the series *Men into Space* (1959–60), and, no doubt thanks to his smooth vocal chords, his became the voice behind many commericals.

In an effort to keep fit while at the same time relaxing, Lundigan, who loved the out-of-doors, liked to play golf and swim. Far from bland offscreen, his verve and enthusiasm kept him more than busy with family, work, play, and charity activities until his death in 1975.

Peleliu

Admiral Nimitz's Central Pacific "island-hopping" campaign was directed toward the China-Luzon-Formosa triangle. If successful, it would position the Allied forces within reach of the Japanese islands, for a decisive showdown against a weakened enemy.

But Gen. Douglas MacArthur, supreme commander of Allied Forces in the Southwest Pacific, opposed the strategy. He went so far as to state in the *New York Times,* 22 September 1943: "Island hopping . . . is not my idea of how to end the war as soon and as cheaply as possible."

MacArthur directed his armies to drive instead through Southwest Asia, cutting off the flow of Japanese war materials. En route, he realized his goal of liberating the Philippines. MacArthur insisted that a full invasion of the Philippines must take place. Not only had he promised to return, he argued, but also if he failed to do so, thousands of Filipino guerrillas fighting the Japanese would suffer greatly, as would the American prisoners of war being held on Luzon. Further, if the islands were not liberated as quickly as possible, it would appear that the United States had once again abandoned the Philippine people.

While the island-hopping debate continued at the Combined Chiefs of Staff level, planes from Task Force 38 carriers struck the central Philippines. The results surprised nearly everyone: the forces of Adm. William Frederick "Bull" Halsey, Jr., lost eight aircraft while destroying a dozen freighters and two hundred Japanese planes. Now convinced that the central Philippines was a weak and poorly defended stronghold, Halsey recommended that the invasion of outlying Japanese islands (which had been considered as possible staging bases for an attack on Leyte) be abandoned. Instead, he argued, the amphibious forces and manpower should be given to MacArthur for his invasion of Leyte.

Accordingly, Nimitz ordered the invasion fleet for Yap island to report to MacArthur's headquarters in the Admiralty Islands, and all plans to invade outlying islands were dropped. But neither Nimitz nor the Joint Chiefs gave such an order to the Palau-bound forces: they believed that Peleliu was a critical staging base for the Leyte operation. Thus, American forces invaded the island on 15 September 1944.

Peleliu was defended by 10,500 elite Japanese troops, many of them veterans of the fighting in China. Their commander, Col. Kunio Nakagawa, and the Japanese higher command had learned many valuable lessons from the Saipan invasion. They now changed their tactics to inflict the most casualties on the invaders and, perhaps, hold the island. Instead of trying to repel the Marines on the beaches, they withdrew to fortifications farther inland, fortifications that were interconnected through tunnels and caves. They positioned their pillboxes and firing points strategically, from sheltered, almost impenetrable caverns. The Marines would have to dig them out at a high cost.

The heroics of the Marines who fought at Peleliu are legendary in the Corps. Pfc. Arthur J. Jackson became a one-man army, storming one enemy position after another with grenades and gunfire. In all, he single-handedly destroyed twelve pillboxes and fifty Japanese defenders. Jackson received a battlefield commission and was later awarded the Medal of Honor. Seven other Marines also received the Medal of Honor, six of them posthumously, for throwing their bodies on live grenades to save their comrades.

Troops from the Army's 321st Infantry, 81st Infantry Division, were ordered to relieve the decimated 1st Marine Division. They joined the 5th and 7th Marines in the final assault operations. But on 15 October, one month after the invasion, the Japanese still held an area measuring four hundred by five hundred yards.

The battle dragged on through the last days of November, well after MacArthur had returned to the Philippines in glory. Even then, organized bands of die-hard Japanese continued to hold out in Peleliu's trackless caverns until 1946.

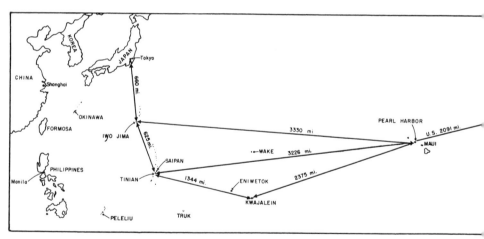

Pacific Ocean areas. (Marine Corps Historical Center)

Okinawa

Okinawa was the last big battle that the Marines fought in the Pacific. Taking the island positioned the Allied forces closer to the Japanese home islands and ensured continuous air coverage for the eventual invasion of Japan. Admiral Spruance commanded the invasion force, which included the U.S. 5th Fleet and the 10th Army (three Marine divisions, four Army divisions). The invading force, the 10th Army, consisted of two Marine divisions, the 1st and 6th, and two Army infantry divisions, the 7th and 96th.

The Japanese troops, here under the command of Lt. Gen. Mitsuru Ushijima, allowed the invading forces to land unopposed. In fact, there was no contention at all for the two airfields located at the center of the sixty-mile-long island. Ushijima's 32d Army formed its defense in the mountainous terrain at the southern end of the island. Rocky cross-island ridges hid tunnels, caves, and entrenched mortars positioned along reverse slopes. The invaders were forced to fight their way slowly, through well-fortified installations, against an enemy who was prepared to fight to the last man.

In their grueling drive across Okinawa, Marines had to fight their way slowly, against a well-prepared enemy who fought to the death.

Marines sight-in on one of the many bitterly contested cave positions throughout Okinawa's hills and ridges. Here, they have just thrown in an explosive charge and wait to see if enemy soldiers will try to escape.

It was General Ushijima's hope that by delaying American forces on Okinawa, Japanese bombers and kamikazes would be able to weaken the supporting Allied fleet to the point that the invaders could no longer sustain a continued assault on the island. It was a plan that could well have worked.

But Americans fought Ushijima's army and the Japanese air fleet with overwhelming land, sea, and air power, in the end winning the day. By the time the campaign was over, the 10th Army had suffered 7,613 killed and missing, with 31,807 wounded. The Marine Corps had sustained 20,020 casualties, 3,561 of them killed in action.

The Navy was hit hardest. Japanese bombers and 1,900 kamikazes sank 36 ships (12 destroyers were lost), damaged 368 other ships, and downed 763 U.S. aircraft. The Navy suffered 4,907 men killed, with 4,800 wounded and missing in action. The Japanese suffered 142,000 casualties, among whom 107,539 were killed.

Jock Mahoney

enowned stuntman Jock Mahoney worked his way into acting
after doubling in dangerous scenes for actors such as Errol
Flynn, Gregory Peck, and Randolph Scott, in films including
the *Durango Kid* Westerns and many, many others. When he eventually was cast in small roles in early films, he did his own stunts, often
saving the studio the expense of hiring a stuntman.

A native of Chicago (17 February 1919), as a young man Jacques
O'Mahoney was disciplined and superbly conditioned, not afraid of
taking risks. At the University of Iowa, he became an Amateur Athletic Union swimming champion, and after college, the star athlete
worked with thoroughbred horses.

After 8 December 1941, when the United States declared war on
Japan—and then Germany and Italy, as Japan's allies, declared war on

the United States on 11 December—O'Mahoney offered to become a civilian instructor for the Army Air Corps, where he taught young cadets for a year. In early 1943 he enlisted in the Marine Corps, and was sent to San Diego for recruit training.

He received his Navy wings at Pensacola, Florida, on 5 December 1944, at the rank of sergeant. He was then sent to the Marine Fighter Operational Training Unit at Naval Air Station Jacksonville, where he was certified as a naval aviation pilot on 6 May 1945. That August he was still attached to the unit, flying F4U Corsairs. The war was almost over, and Jacques O'Mahoney never did get to the fleet to fight the enemy; instead, he remained in training until the end of the war. When he was discharged in late 1945 from the Marine Corps, he wore a technical sergeant's stripes and naval aviator's wings.

With his military service ended, Jacques O'Mahoney decided to pursue the acting profession. But his postwar plan did not go smoothly: despite the acting lessons that he took in Hollywood, O'Mahoney's natural abilities in dramatic interpretation left much to be desired. He did manage to parlay his way into a few bit parts in low-budget Westerns, but his self-consciousness was clear to all, including himself. Nevertheless, show business still appealed to him, and he looked for a niche in it. What were his strong points? Could he use them in this field? His horse savvy, his athletic prowess, and his outstanding physical condition were definite pluses. Surely they could be used somehow.

Thus O'Mahoney became a stuntman in a myriad of the Westerns being produced at the time. He was quoted in a *Leatherneck* article ("Colt, Mare's Leg, and Derringer," July 1960) as saying, "I guess I fell off every horse in Hollywood."

Not only did he fall off horses, he also jumped horses off cliffs into the water, got hanged, was buried in a mine shaft, dived down staircases, and jumped out of moving trains. He suffered broken bones more than once. After he'd taken these beatings for a while, Gene Autry took notice of the multiskilled and extremely handsome young man of chiseled features, perhaps sympathizing with his predicament—or perhaps realizing that he could save some money.

He began to give the stuntman small parts in his pictures. Mahoney dropped the O' and turned Jacques into Jock, common practice in those days of Anglicizing all names. He handled himself well, so Autry signed him on to star in 105 episodes of the rousing TV series *Range Rider* (1951–53). This work was far preferable to risking his life all the time. Even though he still performed his own stunts, at least he no longer did much of all Hollywood's. It represented a good beginning for Mahoney, who developed his acting skills as his self-consciousness dissipated.

Westerns in which he appeared include *The Fighting Frontiersman* (1947), *The Blazing Trail* (1949), *The Texas Rangers* (1951), *The Kid from Broken Gun* (1952), *Showdown at Abilene* (1956), and *Joe Dakota* (1957). After Universal-International Pictures signed him, he was cast in many roles beyond the Western range. He appeared in three Tarzan films, starring in the latter two (and thus becoming the thirteenth onscreen King of the Jungle): *Tarzan the Magnificent,* 1960; *Tarzan Goes to India,* 1962; and *Tarzan's Three Challenges,* 1963.

Other films he made include *The Walls of Hell* (1964), *Runaway Girl* (1966), *The Glory Stompers* (1967), *Bandolero* (1968), *Tom* (1973), *The Bad Bunch* (1976), and *The End* (1978). Jock Mahoney's television credits include the *Loretta Young Theater, Wagon Train,* and *Yancy Derringer* (1958–59), in which he played the post–Civil War bon vivant.

He acted in many more shows (*Rawhide, Batman, Tarzan, Daniel Boone,* among others) before a 1973 stroke forced him to slow down—but not to stop. Programs such as *Streets of San Francisco, B.J. and the Bear, The Fall Guy,* and *Simon and Simon* followed. Mahoney was married to Maggie Field and was the stepfather of actress Sally Field. He died in 1989.

Ed McMahon

The straight man on the *Tonight Show Starring Johnny Carson* got his early training by watching his father, Edward McMahon, Sr., as he ran bingo games and fortune wheels at carnivals. Edward Leo Peter McMahon, Jr. (born in Detroit on 6 March 1923), idolized his father, with his class, and his charm, and his strong character.

His parents moved every year, because of Senior's work. In summers while they were on the circuit, they left their only child with his grandmother, Katie Fitzgerald McMahon, in Lowell, Massachusetts, near Boston. He liked to listen to his grandfather's home-built radio, which picked up Pittsburgh's KDKA announcer Paul Douglas on the *Fred Waring Show*. The junior McMahon was fascinated by that smooth, intelligent voice, which imparted knowledge while conveying the certainty to its listeners that the origin of those sound waves was a real, live person.

Young Ed pretended he, too, was a radio announcer. In his grandparents' living room, while playing the Victrola for background music and speaking into a flashlight-microphone, he broadcast his program to the attentive audience of his dog. Soon, trained to be a hustler from earliest youth, Ed realized that the real person who was delivering programs to audiences in living rooms throughout the land was not, necessarily, all that different from himself. That silvery voice could be his someday, with the proper preparation.

His grandmother convinced his parents to let the boy stay in Lowell for his final high-school years, and he attended Olney High School there. Meanwhile, by age fifteen he was announcing at carnivals; by seventeen he was given his own bingo truck and crew to manage. He was sent on the road as the mike man who called the games. His calling out of bingo numbers turned out to be more good training for his stagelike projection of an authoritarian voice.

Thus Ed McMahon and his voice matured, as he sprouted up to three inches over six feet. He wanted to go to college, and that cost money that his family did not have. So he took a construction job and started taking elocution classes at Boston's Emerson College, preparing to follow Paul Douglas on the airwaves. With the funding finally in order, he started at Boston College, majoring in electrical engineering.

But in the meantime, the United States had gotten into World War II, and McMahon, like so many others, wanted to get into it too. He wanted to be a fighter pilot in the Marines. He enrolled in the Navy's V-5 program for aviation cadets, with the strategy of someday receiving a commission and transferring into the Marine Corps.

After completing the program, McMahon returned to Lowell while he waited for the Navy to determine his future. He used his microphone background to get a broadcasting job with local radio station WLLH. Every night from six in the evening until one in the morning, the tones of Ed McMahon's voice traveled over the airwaves into living rooms, bringing news, sports, weather, and interviews.

He also parlayed his way into a job as a civil engineer's assistant, through the War Department. After convincing the assistant crew chief that he could learn the job quickly, McMahon spent his days enlarging an Army Air Corps field near Bedford, Massachusetts. That job proved to be useful in more ways than the obvious: dollars at the McMahon house were chronically stretched to the limits of their endurance, and McMahon was able to surprise his parents at Christmas with a tree that he chopped down while working on extending a runway.

Six weeks later, Ed McMahon was called to active duty. Having completed two years at Boston College, he qualified for the Navy's flight program as a naval aviation cadet. Among the group of 150 students who left Boston together that year, McMahon was one of only two who eventually received their wings. The others either washed out along the way or quit the program—and a few were killed in training accidents.

Repeatedly selected to serve as cadet regimental commander, no doubt due to his authoritative voice and his tallness, McMahon disliked being singled out and having to play the boss. Nevertheless, he carried out his orders while managing, for the most part, to remain on his fellow cadets' good side. He went through flight training at Texarkana flying Piper Cubs. Next stop was Denton, Texas, and his third and final flight school was at the University of Georgia in Athens, where he received still more training and screening.

At last he was selected to proceed to Pensacola, there to begin his first real step toward winning his Navy wings. Upon receiving these, McMahon applied for and was accepted into the Marine Corps. He was assigned to a Marine fighter command and reported to his first active-duty station, at Lee Field, Jacksonville, Florida. Here McMahon trained in his first combatant aircraft, the gull-winged F4U Corsair fighter.

Any day, McMahon fully expected to be assigned to a replacement squadron that would be sent to the Pacific. But instead he was ordered to serve as a flight instructor. Studying furiously to stay one lesson ahead of his students, Ed McMahon spent the next twenty-two months at Lee, teaching and flight-testing new aircraft. During this long tour he married Alyce Ferrell, and the newlyweds wasted no time in starting their family.

Then, on the day when he finally received the long-expected orders to join a fighter squadron on the West Coast, the Americans dropped the bomb. With the war over, McMahon's orders were canceled. He was ordered to join Marine Air Group (MAG 91), Marine Fighter Squadron 911 (VMF-911), at the Marine Corps Auxiliary Air Field at Kinston, North Carolina.

This was one of several outlying fields under the command of the Marine Air Station at Cherry Point, North Carolina. VMF 911 was composed mostly of F4U Corsairs and, later, F7F Tigercats. It was a replacement training squadron, and McMahon was once again flying Corsairs as an instructor. He remained at Kinston until he was discharged from active duty, in February 1946. He then elected to remain in the Marine Corps Reserve; and it would be just a few years until the Marine Corps recalled him to active duty, to assume flight duties during the Korean War.

After World War II, McMahon completed his undergraduate work at Catholic University in Washington, D.C. He used his father's connections to land a job on the Atlantic City boardwalk, selling pens and vegetable slicers. After enrolling in school, he and another student also opened a clothes-cleaning service, which helped to support his family while he was in school. McMahon finally received his B.A. from Catholic University in 1949 with a major in speech and drama.

Following graduation, he got a job in Philadelphia, at radio station WCAU. The station was just at the point where it was ready to venture into television, which definitely put McMahon in the right place at the right time. He became known to local viewers as Mr. Television. First was the three-hour variety show *The Take Ten Show*; then a morning program *Strictly for the Girls*, which McMahon wrote and produced. Next came the cooking show *Aunt Molly and Ed*; and then *The Silent Service,* imparting the lore of submarines.

On the Saturday circus show *The Big Top*, Ed McMahon played a clown. By 1951, CBS planned for that show (which opened with a shot of McMahon's bald dome presenting the show's title) to be broadcast nationally, while *Strictly for the Girls* would become a regional program. McMahon's career was looking rosy indeed, when he was recalled to active duty for the Korean War in July 1951.

By now, he and Alyce had two children. Captain McMahon

reported to the Naval Air Station at Willow Grove, Pennsylvania, on 16 July 1951. After six weeks there, he was ordered to the Third Marine Air Wing at Miami, as a public information officer. But shortly after his arrival in Miami, his mother, who had heart problems and had worried about him all through World War II, passed away at his parents' home in Atlantic City. McMahon feared that the renewed distress about him had contributed to her untimely demise. Nevertheless, after the funeral he had no choice but to press on and carry out his duty, leaving his father with his pals in Atlantic City, and Alyce and the children with her family in LaCoochey, Florida.

He shipped out for Korea, where he was assigned to the First Marine Air Wing flying unarmed Cessna 180 observation planes. Ed McMahon flew eighty-five missions in Korea, spotting enemy artillery positions and troop movements while dodging fire from below—everything from sidearms to antiaircraft guns. For carrying out these duties successfully, he earned six air medals.

When he was not in the air, in his capacity as public information officer McMahon volunteered to work as the mess-hall officer. His hope was to improve the dismal food and the depressing atmosphere, thereby enhancing the air wing's low morale. His plan worked: he reorganized and spruced up, installed different lights, ordered new supplies, even gave the local children chewing gum and candy bars in return for picking flowers to go on the tables. McMahon applied his homey touch first to the enlisted men's club, then to the officers' club, and finally, by popular demand, to the noncommissioned officers' club. By the time he was finished, the mess hall offered eggs cooked to order, steaks, and French fries; both the O and NCO clubs featured casinos and fifteen-cent martinis—warm ones: lack of ice was the clubs' only major problem.

Even the entertainment improved: with his communications background, McMahon was put in charge of armed-forces radio station Mercury, from which he broadcast at night. Truce talks had begun in July 1951, and a cease-fire was finally declared two years later. In the meantime, McMahon was sometimes able to spend his days watching porpoises from his air mattress as he floated around the Yellow Sea. Even so, he was anxious to return home to see his family, which now included a new baby, and to continue with his show-business career.

McMahon, as a member of the First Marine Air Wing's observation squadron, flew unarmed observation Cessna 180s over Korea. (Photofest)

So he drafted a letter to his commanding officer. He pointed out that his usefulness in Korea was doubtful at best, what with the truce talks dragging on. He requested to be returned to the States and discharged so that he could resume his career. The letter was disapproved all the way up the chain of command.

But when it reached a higher authority, the request was approved. Although McMahon suspected friends in the right places, he never was certain. Per standard procedure, he flew home jumping aboard flight hops across the Pacific, Korea to Tokyo to Guam to Mobile. McMahon returned to Treasure Island in August 1952 and was honorably discharged from the Corps that same month.

Returning to Philadelphia with Alyce and the children, he went straight back to television. He appeared on *The Big Top, Five Minutes More,* and a late-night talk show, *McMahon and Company.* But he wanted to infiltrate the New York market, and he attacked the prob-

This training version of the Corsair was used by the Marine Corps in 1946, when McMahon was an instructor at Kinston Airfield, a subsidiary air base of MCAS Cherry Point.

lem like a military operation. Going into the city each day, he spent hours contacting acquaintances and potential sponsors, anyone who might be able to help him in his two-pronged mission: to find a spot for himself in a network program, and to start making well-paying commercials.

Finally, fate intervened. Dick Clark of *American Bandstand,* who lived next door to the McMahons, was interviewed one day in his apartment. After the work was over, a party spontaneously sprang up for the crew and Clark, with McMahon acting as the master of ceremonies. Clark's producer, noticing the MC's ease and grace with his duties, later suggested to another producer that he consider him for *Who Do You Trust?*

The New York–based show had recently lost its announcer, and McMahon promptly agreed to interview with its star, Johnny Carson. They hit it off immediately, and McMahon began to act as master of ceremonies for the show in October 1958. In 1962, when Carson took over the *Tonight Show* upon Jack Paar's departure, he insisted on bringing McMahon along, and the two remained a team until the last *Tonight Show Starring Johnny Carson,* in 1992.

Carson's sidekick has stayed very busy, aside from his work on that show: he's hosted many television specials, including *Kraft Music Hall* programs, *America's Junior Miss Pageant,* and the Macy's Christmas Day Parade. He's cohosted the annual *Jerry Lewis Muscular Dystrophy Telethon.* He's hosted TV programs such as *Star Search* and *TV's Bloopers and Practical Jokes.*

He's also appeared in plays, including Broadway's *The Impossible Years* and summer stock productions of *Wildcat, Guys and Dolls,* and *Annie Get Your Gun.* In movies, he has acted in, among others, *The Incident* (1967), *Slaughter's Big Rip-Off* (1973), and *Fun with Dick and Jane* (1977). He has also widely traveled the nightclub and college circuits, and he has recorded albums. And he got to make those lucrative commercials, too, for Breck shampoo, Budweiser beer, Cheer detergent, and several other products.

Alyce and Ed were separated in 1972 and divorced in 1976. He then married Victoria Valentine, with whom he had one child; they later divorced. Ed is now married to Pamela McMahon.

He retired from the Marine Corps Reserve as a full colonel, and in 1982 he was named a brigadier general in the California National Guard. When he hasn't been busy with Johnny Carson or plays or movies or television shows or commercials, Ed McMahon has managed his various business and civic involvements, which include managing talent and helping to run a film company committed to environmental concerns. Typically, he flies between at least two states during a workday. A man who loves his work, he likes to be personally present, just to make certain everything is being done the right way.

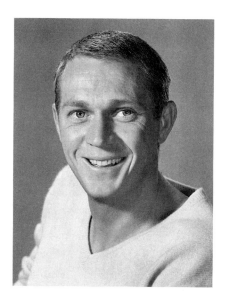

Steve McQueen

Bad boy Steven Terrence McQueen grew up to be a multitalented and tormented man. He was driven toward both glory and self-annihilation. His father abandoned his young bride and son soon after the baby's arrival, on 24 March 1930, in Beach Grove, Indiana, outside of Indianapolis. By the time Steve was three years old, his mother, Julia Ann Crawford McQueen, had left him to live on a farm in Slater, Missouri, with his great-granduncle. He grew close to the reserved yet affectionate Uncle Claude, who took him to movies in town on Saturdays, bought him a tricycle when he was four, and remained the only family with whom he would maintain lasting ties.

The routine of doing chores on the farm, helping Uncle Claude herd the hogs to market, walking to school, and doing his homework kept young Steve busy, if also wondering why his parents had left him. After milking the cows in purple mornings, he would sometimes stretch out in the hay, dozing as the day came awake. When he was twelve, Julia yanked him away (as she'd done once already, then returned him) to bring him back to Beach Grove, then Los Angeles.

She married a man who clearly resented the boy's presence and often beat him, with Julia standing by apparently helpless, for which Steve would never forgive her and for which Julia buried her guilt in alcohol. To escape the home front, the furious, strong-headed adolescent preferred to hang out on the streets. There he fell in with the local gangs, and, with the goal of eventually leading one of them, he pursued his delinquent duties with fervor. After he was nailed for stealing hubcaps off expensive cars, Julia, encouraged by her husband, packed him off to reform school: the California Junior Boys' Republic, Chino.

Strangely, this action helped the defiant lad, after several escape attempts, thanks to the intervention of the school's compassionate superintendent, Mr. Panter. He realized that the only way to reach the young rebel was to reason with him. Did he want to ruin his life? He did not have to. He was intelligent and he could do something with himself, if he was willing to make the effort. Steve listened and understood. He began to work in the shop, learning both skills and self-respect. But on holidays he was left, often alone, at the school.

Julia, meanwhile, was learning a skill too (drafting; she would find employment with North American Aviation), so that she would never again have to rely on a man. Then, fortuitously, her abusive husband died. Free, she moved to New York's Greenwich Village, where, surrounded by other young nonconformists and bohemians, Julia finally felt like she could openly be herself. Later, her son would feel the same way about the Village.

In 1946, apparently feeling that ninth-grader Steve should be with his mother, she took him out of Chino and brought him to New York. Far from forgetting the institution that helped him, McQueen would later help to support it and would periodically visit the boys there, hoping to inspire them do something with their lives, as he himself was inspired to do with his. He also remembered the school in his will, and in 1983 a grateful Boys' Republic opened the Steve McQueen Recreation Center.

Providing a beacon for kids was apparently something McQueen must have felt strongly about, for in 1979 he granted a by-then rare interview to the Alexander Hamilton High School newspaper, the *Federalist,* explaining simply, "I do have a certain respect for youth." First wife Neile McQueen already knew that about him: throughout the tumultuous years as their relationship disintegrated, he always stayed on rock-solid ground where his children were concerned.

He was all too familiar with the lack of such dependability in his own life. In New York, his reunion with his mother was not a pleasant one, and soon the sixteen-year-old decided that from here on, he would go it alone. Predictably, the good-looking youth met an interesting assortment of people in the city, through some of whom he got his first job—on board the tanker *Alpha,* bound for the West Indies. But by the time they reached the Dominican Republic, Steve had had enough of deck scrubbing and garbage hauling. He left the ship at Santo Domingo and found work in a whorehouse as a towel boy, a job that came with benefits: the women took a liking to him and decided to complete the boy's education.

He eventually made his way back to the States, to Port Arthur, Texas, where he worked in another brothel as a waiter, then in Waco and Corpus Christi oil fields, then in a lumber town, then in a carnival. His seventeenth year found the wanderer in Myrtle Beach, South Carolina, where he reached the conclusion that he needed some stability in his life, something he could rely on. On 28 April 1947, in New York City, Steve McQueen enlisted in the Marine Corps.

He was assigned to the 2d Recruit Battalion, Marine Corps Recruit Depot, Parris Island. After boot training, in August he was ordered, as a rifleman, to C Company, 1st Battalion, 4th Marine Regiment, Fleet Marine Force, at Camp Lejeune. A month later he was ordered to the 2d Amphibian Tractor Battalion, FMF, still at Camp Lejeune, where he was a crewman. On 18 September 1947, he became Private First Class McQueen.

But the private first class did not adjust easily to the demanding life of a Marine. He was still (and always would be) a rebel, and he tested the Corps with his antics. In experiences that he probably drew on for his later roles in *The Great Escape* and *Papillon*, he got thrown in the brig for going AWOL after extending a weekend's leave to a leisurely week in the pleasant company of a woman, and then thrown in again

McQueen took great pride in his assignment to security detail for President Truman's yacht, the *Sequoia*. (U.S. Navy)

for a similar caper. Before his three years' enlistment were up, McQueen was busted several times from private first class back to private.

Eventually he did shape up, though, and loved his Marine Corps life. His time in the service not only built on the sense of discipline and self-respect that Uncle Claude and Mr. Panter had tried to instill in him, it also gave him the confidence to continue developing his mechanical skills. Another thing he enjoyed was the excellent physical condition that it required one to maintain, and McQueen would keep this up for most of his adult life, with rigorous daily workouts.

One prank that foreshadowed his later racing career was trying to soup up a tank engine so he could drive the fastest tank in his unit. Using his mechanical know-how and the help of his buddies, McQueen worked on the overhaul until the engine blew. But at least it was a learning experience for him: tank engines were not meant for speed conversion.

Assigned in November 1947 to the Amphibian Tractor Company, 22d Marines (Reinforced), FMF, Quantico, Virginia, McQueen worked as a tank and amphibious tractor crewman. With this unit, he participated in cold-weather training operations in Labrador, Canada, where, one day, one of the amphibian tanks capsized in the frigid waters. With big waves crashing over them and their futures looking increasingly bleak with every stormy sweep, the crew clung to the steel hull. Pfc. Steve McQueen raced his amphibian tractor to the rescue, maneuvered close to the tank, and pulled the endangered Marines to safety.

In September 1948, he was transferred to the 1st Guard Company at the Naval Gun Factory in Washington, D.C. During this tour he was posted as a member of the Honor Guard, tasked with an assignment in which he took great pride: providing security for President Truman's yacht, the *Sequoia*. In May 1949, he returned to the 2d Amphibian Tractor Battalion at Camp Lejeune and served with the unit until his honorable discharge on 27 April 1950.

Still definitely on the wild side, McQueen now at least felt equipped to cope with an uncertain future. Out of the service with little money, he drifted for a while from job to job, driving a cab in D.C. and then settling in Greenwich Village, where, as Julia had years earlier, he felt like he fit in. He worked as a delivery man and bag loader, recapped tires, cut leather for sandal makers, and won at poker (which he'd learned to do in the Corps). For the winter he and a buddy went south to Miami, where they found work as beachboys in a resort hotel. Back in New York the following spring, McQueen took stock of himself and decided to learn a trade using the GI Bill.

An actress friend thought he might have talent—he definitely had a unique look and air about him. At her urging, he agreed to meet with Neighborhood Playhouse director Sanford Meisner. Meisner evidently saw something in the young man too and gave him a bit part in a Yiddish play, then accepted him into the program. McQueen himself was highly dubious about both his ability and the business in general; nevertheless, he persisted. If he was going to do this, he would give it his best shot.

His early acting days were difficult, and he never would become completely comfortable in front of a camera. To supplement his income he found various jobs, bartending and driving a truck. He also discovered motorcycle racing and a love of speed that would last all his life; eventually he became a respected race-car driver at the international-competition level.

McQueen continued to develop his acting skills at the Actor's Studio, working in summer stock and touring with Melvyn Douglas in *Time Out for Ginger.* In 1956 he appeared on Broadway in *The Gep,* then replaced Ben Gazzara for the lead in *A Hatful of Rain,* winning critics' notice. That same year he got a small part in the film *Somebody Up There Likes Me,* and two years later he got a major break when he was cast as Josh Randall in the television series *Wanted—Dead or Alive,* which aired until 1961.

That series made his a household name. By the early 1960s, Steve McQueen had appeared in numerous films, including *The Blob* (1958), *The Great St. Louis Bank Robbery* (1959), *The Magnificent Seven* (1960), *Hell Is for Heroes* (1962), *The War Lover* (1962), and *Love with the Proper Stranger* (1963). *The Great Escape* (1963) established him as a major star, after which his popularity continued to soar, and by 1969, his clear, piercing eyes, behind which something was always brewing, had helped make him one of the most beloved stars in the world.

His many memorable contributions to American cinema include *The Cincinnati Kid* (1965), *Nevada Smith* (1966), *The Sand Pebbles* (1966, for which he was nominated for an Academy Award), *The Thomas Crown Affair* (1968), *Bullitt* (1968), *The Reivers* (1969), *Junior Bonner* (1972), *Papillon* (1973), and *The Towering Inferno* (1974).

The former lonely Missouri farm boy had plenty of company now, and he reveled in being a superstar. But wealth and status came with problems of their own—and temptations that McQueen had no desire to resist. Like a hungry kid who'd been handed ten dollars and sent on his own to a candy store, he wanted everything he saw.

By 1970 his wife (since 1956), dancer Neile Adams, could no longer bear his new life-style and excesses. Adams, who at age eleven had been interned with her mother in the Japanese concentration camp Santo Tomas in the Philippines (both survived), had two children with McQueen. She and Steve remained close for the rest of his life, but in 1972 they were divorced. McQueen was married twice more, to actress Ali McGraw from 1973 to 1978, and to model Barbara Minty in 1980.

He had begun to seek calmer pleasures by the late seventies, buying a ranch in Santa Paula, California, and avidly collecting American memorabilia, including gas pumps, jukeboxes, antique toys, and classic motorcycles and cars. He got his pilot's license and soon had a small collection of antique planes, including a 1940s PT-17 Stearman, which he flew in a 1929 flying suit. He also owned a 1946 L-4 H Piper and a 1931 Pitcairn PA-8 biplane. Steve McQueen lived many exhilarating moments up there in the endless azure before dying in 1980 at age fifty. Long-term exposure to the asbestos in brake linings and fireproof racing suits was suspected to have caused his lung cancer, not helped by his smoking.

Hugh O'Brian

B orn 19 April 1925 in Rochester, New York, to a Marine father
(retired Capt. John Krampe, who served as adjutant of the 9th
Infantry Battalion in Chicago), Hugh Charles Krampe soon
became interested in a military career of his own. Taught all three stan-
zas of the Marines's Hymn and how to field-strip a weapon, he often
accompanied the captain's unit to summer camp at Great Lakes, Illinois, where fathers who were drilling often brought their sons along.
The Pup Marines, as they were called, formed their own units and did
their best to emulate the larger Marines.

John Krampe, a tenacious yet patient and gentle disciplinarian, did
his best to inculcate in his two boys the goal of excellence, in both their
own achievements and those of others. Working as a sales executive,
he moved frequently, taking wife Edith and their Pup Marines with

(Hugh O'Brian collection)

Private First Class Krampe *(top right)* with his father, Capt. John Krampe, USMC; brother, Don, who later served with the 1st Marine Division in Korea (where he was wounded); and mother, Edith. (Hugh O'Brian collection)

him. After Rochester the family moved to Pennsylvania and then Long Island before arriving in Chicago.

By that time Hugh was a teenager, and during his junior-high-school years, his parents agreed to let him attend the Roosevelt Military Academy in Aledo, Illinois. From there he moved on to Kemper Military School, Boonville, Missouri, and then to the University of Cincinnati, which his father had attended before him.

Drill instructor Pfc. H. C. Krampe sits in middle left front row, with no rifle and his tie windblown.

But World War II put a stop to that: on 14 May 1943, Hugh enlisted in the Marines. His previous military training paid off when, at the age of eighteen, he became one of the youngest drill instructors in the Corps. The senior Krampe definitely supplied his fair share of new Marines, with both of his sons joining the Corps. Hugh's brother, Don, would later be wounded in Korea while with the 1st Marine Division; he was released from active duty after serving three years.

Hugh went through basic training at the Recruit Depot, San Diego, with the 3d Recruit Battalion. Asked to box for his platoon, he met actor John Wayne, who wanted to be a Marine but had never been able to pass the rigorous physical exam because of his football injuries. Wayne refereed the bout, in what would become the beginning of a friendship that lasted for the rest of Wayne's life. With their lives intertwining at regular intervals, the two finally costarred in *The Shootist* (1976), Wayne's last movie. Thus, Hugh O'Brian became the last man ever to be shot by John Wayne.

But in 1943, it was Private Krampe who was doing the shooting. On the range at Camp Matthews, he shot expert and was chosen as the honor graduate. Promoted to private first class, he joined 3d

Casual Company, Marine Corps Recruit Depot, on 9 July 1943. Next assigned to the 28th Marines (part of the 5th Marine Division at Camp Pendleton), Krampe became a tank crewman. Serving in B Company of the 5th Tanks, he worked hard to prove himself as his unit prepared to invade Iwo Jima.

That unit did lose about 80 percent of its men at Iwo, but Hugh was not among them. Before their departure he was pulled out of the unit and rerouted, to attend the Naval Academy Preparatory School, Naval Training Center, Bainbridge, Maryland. Hugh Krampe was enrolled there from 7 October 1944 to 28 June 1945, while attached to Barracks Detachment, Marine Barracks, at the Navy Yard in Washington, D.C.

By the time Krampe was working on acceptance into the Naval Academy, Germany had surrendered unconditionally, and he had reconsidered his plan for a life of military service. He finished out his enlistment in several U.S. locations: on 29 June 1945 he joined the 1st Casual Company, Headquarters Battalion, Camp Lejeune; from there, he underwent a series of transfers that bounced him around the country from Camp Pendleton in Oceanside, California, back to the East Coast in 1946. He was assigned to the U.S. Naval Gun Factory, Washington, D.C., and promoted to corporal on 6 September 1946. That December, he was sent to the Separation Center, Great Lakes.

Upon his 1947 honorable discharge at Great Lakes (with a Good Conduct Medal), Hugh headed back to his family and began appearing in local theater productions. On 30 October 1947 he joined the Organized Marine Corps Reserve, 13th Infantry Battalion, USMCR, Santa Monica, California, reappointed as a corporal. He remained in the Reserves until 29 October 1949, when he was discharged in Los Angeles.

Back in civilian life, one needed to earn money. Hugh worked at odd jobs—sales, landscaping, collecting garbage. He spent a summer in Los Angeles, with plans for law school. But when an actor friend fell ill and asked him to take his place, Hugh liked the experience so much that he changed career paths again. He began to study acting at UCLA, performing with small theater groups in the area. Sometimes using the stage name Jaffer Gray, he eventually settled on Hugh O'Brian.

It was about a year later that Ida Lupino saw him perform. Impressed with O'Brian's voice and his strong, chiseled features, she signed him on for a film that she was directing: *Never Fear* (1950). Universal-International Studios then offered him a contract, and between 1951 and 1954, O'Brian made more than twenty films, including *Little Big Horn* (1951), *The Raiders* (1952), and *Seminole* (1953). By 1954, *Fireman, Save My Child* won him favorable critical attention, and the following year he began starring on television as Wyatt Earp, marshal of Dodge City, Kansas.

He was hand-picked for that job by Earp's biographer, Stuart Lake, who also created the program *Life and Legend of Wyatt Earp*. Shortly after the show debuted in 1955 as the "first adult Western," breaking the stereotype of the singing cowboy created for kids, it became the top-rated TV show. Wyatt Earp maintained law and order for seven years (until 1961), during which time the show was rated among the viewing public's favorites.

O'Brian's role not only made his a well-known name, it brought a steady, substantial income—almost a thousand dollars a week—as well as more work. The actor put his new affluence to good use: he invested wisely, including in real estate and sporting goods. He became known for his charitable activities, especially the Hugh O'Brian Youth Leadership Program (HOBY), which he started in 1958 after visiting Dr. Albert Schweitzer. O'Brian traveled to Africa to see for himself the famous humanitarian's clinic; nine days later, after joining in the daily volunteer activities, he came away deeply impressed with the doctor's conviction that the young must be taught to think for themselves.

Upon his return to the States, O'Brian promptly formed HOBY, which, forty years later, has become his legacy. Nonprofit and funded entirely through the private sector, its mission is to get outstanding tenth graders together with notable leaders from every field—such as Neil Armstrong, Gerald Ford, Mohammad Ali, Ann Landers, Charles H. Percy, Roger Staubach, and retired Army general W. C. Westmoreland, among others. The objective is to motivate youngsters through a series of seminars, showing them how the thinking process works. They then have two more years of high school in which to put their new skills into effect, hopefully also influencing their classmates to accept responsibility for their own futures. Alumni numbering in the thousands have confirmed that this program in fact was the turning point in their lives.

O'Brian has gone on to make many more movies, including *The Fiend Who Walked the West* (1958), *In Harm's Way* (1965, in which one of the authors of this book, Jim Wise, and his wife appeared as extras), *Doing Time on Planet Earth* (1988), and the TV movie *Wyatt Earp: Return to Tombstone* (1994). He has appeared widely on television, starting with live TV (in 1948 he appeared on *Arch Oboler's Mystery Theatre*), and including *Fireside Theater, Ford Theater, Playhouse 90, Hallmark Hall of Fame,* and *Fantasy Island.* He has also acted in several Broadway plays and has acted in, produced, or coproduced many others.

O'Brian has not forgotten his ties with the Corps. In 1965, during the Vietnam War, he took two parachute jumps in Salt Lake City as a recruiting promotion for the Marines, a stunt for which he got two hours' preparation. He also made three trips to visit the troops, including at Khe Sanh Marine combat base. At the suggestion of President Lyndon B. Johnson, he edited down the Broadway show *Guys and Dolls* to just over an hour's length and recruited the guys—all former GIs—and dolls for the production. They spent five weeks visiting the wounded and performing on hardtops (just twice on real-live stages and twice on carrier decks), averaging three shows a day to grateful audiences of three or four thousand.

Busy as ever, O'Brian has received numerous achievement awards and honorary university degrees. Never married, he shares his home with Virginia Barber, a fashion merchandizer and teacher who also works with teenagers, and their dogs, overlooking Beverly Hills. His favorite pastimes include swimming, scuba diving, and bicycling.

Gerald O'Loughlin

Ｎew York City native Gerald Stuart O'Loughlin was born to
Wall Street corporation lawyer Gerald Senior and *Mayflower*
descendant Laura Ward O'Loughlin on 23 December 1921.
Senior died suddenly when Junior was just six years old, and Laura
moved her son and daughter (Janet, who during World War II would
become a Navy ensign) out to the country.

There they flourished, Gerry raising chickens and making a little
money from them, and learning how not to play with guns. After his
first acting experience in a high-school production, he never again felt
professionally fulfilled until he was able to get back on the stage.

That would not be until many years later; after high school, the duti-
ful son went on to Lafayette College in Easton, Pennsylvania, where he
began work toward a practical, useful degree in mechanical engineer-

(O'Loughlin collection)

ing—and joined a drama club. But World War II made its demands on his conscience too, and on 13 July 1942, O'Loughlin enlisted in the Marines. "I was attracted to the Marine Corps uniform," he told *Leatherneck* magazine (March 1988), but he also remembered an Army uncle who'd regaled him, as a child, with stories about and praise for the Marines he'd served with in World War I.

After spending a year on inactive duty (during which he stayed at Lafayette), he was activated on 1 July 1943, and ordered to boot camp at Parris Island. O'Loughlin actually enjoyed the physical regimen and the wonderful shape it pummeled him into. After that invigorating experience was over, he was ordered to the Navy's V-12 training program at the University of Rochester, New York. Having completed that, he was appointed as an officer candidate and sent to Camp Lejeune, where he kept up his physical fitness, attended numerous operations-oriented lectures, developed his military skills, and received his first promotion, to private first class.

Next came ten weeks of training at Quantico's Officer Candidate Course, which he completed in December 1944. On 1 January 1945, Gerald O'Loughlin was commissioned a second lieutenant, USMCR. Ten weeks of yet more training followed, at the Reserve Officers' School, later known as the Basic School, Quantico. On 22 April 1945, he returned to Camp Lejeune, for training as a platoon commander and combat engineer officer.

O'Loughlin was assigned to the Officer Application Course, which would give him much-needed command time, especially if he was planning to make a career out of all this. In May 1945 he headed to the West Coast, riding the train with the rest of 66th Replacement Draft formed at "Tent City" Lejeune, comprising seven officers and forty-one enlisted men. During the five-day trip across country, O'Loughlin and comrades noticed not only the magnificent countryside, but also, in Texas, trainloads of German prisoners of war. As the war-bound Marines rode south from Los Angeles to Camp Pendleton, the Pacific Coast welcomed them with fruit-tree fragrances wafting off the hills on one side, sea lions barking in the surf on the other.

On 26 May 1945, O'Loughlin's unit shipped out from San Diego aboard the USS *Niagara* (APA-87) to Honolulu, arriving at Pearl Har-

Marines march into a Japanese city for occupation duty, 1945.

bor on 1 June. If one had to be caught in a holding pattern, there were, of course, far worse places than Hawaii for waiting. O'Loughlin, hearing first that they were bound for Okinawa and then that they were not, but instead would invade Japan, passed the days in his new Tent City as best he could, alleviating the tension, in the evenings, with various alcoholic medleys.

More than a month later, in July, he was assigned as platoon commander of 1st Platoon, Company C, with the 2d Engineer Battalion, 5th Marine Division. For the next month they trained for the invasion of Japan . . . until the atomic bomb ended the war, with no invasion. Instead, O'Loughlin was sent to occupy the conquered territory.

On 27 August, 5th Division Marines left Hilo, Hawaii, aboard the USS *Montrose* (APA-212). After taking on supplies and joining a convoy in Pearl Harbor, on 1 September they steamed for Japan, still using wartime zigzag patterns and nighttime blackouts—just in case. The war hadn't been over for long: what if the Japanese had one final trick up their sleeves?

But they arrived safely at Sasebo, on 22 September. O'Loughlin and company spent an uneventful two-plus months' occupation of Japan, until, as "low-point" Marines who had just arrived, they switched places with the combat-weathered "high-point" men of the 2d Marine Divison. The vets were sent home in December, while the low-points waited six months more, until 15 June 1946. O'Loughlin spent the time in Nagasaki, then in the southeastern tip of Kyushu. After that, the 24th Infantry Division, U.S. Army, took over as the occupation force, and O'Loughlin's unit was sent home. He was promoted to first lieutenant during the sea voyage back Stateside.

Released from active duty on 24 October 1946, O'Loughlin remained in the Reserves. He finished his degree in mechanical engineering, but then, still qualifying for two more years on the GI Bill, he enrolled at New York's Neighborhood Playhouse. There he discovered mentor Sanford Meisner and immersed himself in the acting environment that he so preferred to engineering.

Gerald O'Loughlin seemed set on a course toward the acting profession when, in January 1950, he was recalled to active duty. He was not sent to Korea, however—just to Camp Lejeune, where he served with the 2d Marine Division. Discharged in June of that same year, he went back to civilian life and his theatrical ambitions.

This time he studied at New York's Actor's Studio, performing onstage when he could, including in the Broadway plays *A Streetcar Named Desire* and *One Flew over the Cuckoo's Nest*. In 1962 his off-Broadway performance in *Who Will Save the Plowboy* won him an Obie, the annual theater award established in 1955 by the *Village Voice* for off-Broadway (OB) productions.

He began to be offered roles in Hollywood as well, and O'Loughlin has been successfully plying his trade ever since. During much of the 1960s he flew between the two coasts, finally landing in California, where most of the lucrative work was. He has appeared in movies such as *In Cold Blood* (1967, with Robert Blake), *The Organization* (1971, with Sidney Poitier), *The Valachi Papers* (1972, with Charles Bronson), and *Crimes of Passion* (1984, with Kathleen Turner and Anthony Perkins). His myriad television credits include *Ben Casey,*

Naked City, Hawaii Five-O, M.A.S.H., Ironside, The FBI, The Rookies, and *Murder, She Wrote.*

In addition, O'Loughlin directed a few episodes of *The Rookies* and has done quite a bit of teaching, notably at Hollywood's Lee Strasberg Theatre Institute. For fun, in activities that may on occasion put his mechanical-engineering training to use after all, he likes to work with wood and fix up old cars. In 1976 O'Loughlin was divorced from (but remained on friendly terms with) actress and casting director Meryl Abeles, with whom he had two children.

He may have ultimately liked acting best, but his military training was lasting: O'Loughlin has credited it with teaching him, among other essential skills such as how to be part of a team, how to push relentlessly ahead to get the job done, whatever the job may be. And, to keep his Corps sense of camaraderie alive, he belongs to the Marine Corps Combat Correspondents Association and sometimes might be spotted at a Corps birthday party.

George Peppard

The intrepid *A-Team* leader Hannibal Smith of television's popular series (1983–87) started out in plays written by Shakespeare. The only son of light-opera singer Vernelle Rohrer
Peppard and building contractor George Senior, George William
Peppard, Jr., was born in Detroit on 1 October 1928. Successfully
overpowering his mother's determination that he become a concert
pianist, Peppard opted instead for a future in civil engineering.

In high school, he went out for football and track. These were
viewed as manly pursuits, allowing him to retain his virile image, in
the eyes of his Dearborn High classmates, while he also got involved
in the more emotionally exposed field of drama studies. Even more
manly, he enlisted in the Marine Corps straight out of high school,
on 8 July 1946, in Detroit.

(Photofest)

Eighteen-year-old Peppard was dispatched forthwith to Parris Island boot camp, and then, in August, on to Camp Lejeune. There he was assigned to Casual Company, Headquarters and Service Battalion. A month later, in September 1946, he was reassigned to 1st Battalion, 10th Marines, Fleet Marine Force.

On 18 January 1947, Peppard departed Morehead City, North Carolina, aboard the USS LST 912, arriving at Little Creek, Virginia, the next day. Sailing from there on 18 February, again on board LST 912, he took part in Atlantic Fleet Landing Exercises at Culebra, an island off the east coast of Puerto Rico. He returned to Morehead City on the twenty-second of that month.

Promoted to corporal in April 1947, on 10 July he sailed, aboard LST 912, from Morehead City for amphibious rehearsal-training maneuvers in preparation for Exercise CAMID II, from 16 to 26 July 1947. After a week of relaxing, along with more training, in Little Creek at the U.S. Naval Amphibious Base, Peppard reembarked on the LST 912 to participate in Exercise CAMID II, which took place from 11 to 23 August 1947. He was back in Morehead City two days later.

On 10 September he was transferred to Camp Lejeune, where he joined G Battery, 3d Battalion, 10th Marines. He remained with this unit for the remainder of his active-duty service. Eighteen months after enlisting, on 29 January 1948, Corporal Peppard was honorably discharged from the Marine Corps.

He enrolled at Purdue University to pursue his civil-engineering training and continue his drama interests. But when his father suddenly died, he quit to run the family business for a year, finishing up several building contracts that Senior had had under way at the time of his demise.

By now Peppard Junior's dramatic interests were exerting the greater pull on him, and he transferred to the College of Fine Arts of the Carnegie Institute of Technology, Pittsburgh. There he finished his bachelor of arts degree (1955), studied Greek and Shakespearean theater, and acted in the 1952 and 1953 Oregon Shakespeare Festivals. It was in Pittsburgh that George Peppard made his professional debut, in *The Crucible,* presented at the Pittsburgh Playhouse. While at Carnegie, he also put in some hours at a radio station, thanks to which he could add "disk jockey" and "station engineer" to his résumé.

Marines participate in Caribbean training exercise following the end of World War II.

After graduating, he moved to New York to study at the Actor's Studio. Peppard and his bride, Helen Davies (since 1954), lived in Greenwich Village on Bleecker Street, in a cold-water flat that ran them forty dollars a month. To help pay for it, Peppard worked in a bank and drove a cab. Known from the start for expressing his true opinions to agents, producers, and directors alike, Peppard may have been financially challenged, but he refused to accept roles that he considered lesser. Even so, before too long the blond, comely, and natty actor was getting work in both radio and television.

Within his first year in the city, he and two other Actor's Studio graduates, Pat Hingle and Arthur Storch, were selected to appear in the Broadway production of N. Richard Nash's *Girls of Summer*, which opened in November 1956. Though the play bombed, Peppard was singled out for critical approval. Dauntless, the Actor's Studio trio went on to work together again, in Peppard's first movie, *The Strange One* (1957). Again Peppard was noticed, but nothing happened to his career as a result. Now he was seriously concerned, and he took a short break to reevaluate his career choice.

But acting won out again, and Peppard came back to television work in the *Hallmark Hall of Fame* and *Suspicion*. Another Broadway role came his way in 1958's *The Pleasure of His Company*, which was a critical success. On next to Hollywood, he was cast in movies including *Pork Chop Hill* (1959, starring Gregory Peck), *Home from the Hill* (1960, starring Robert Mitchum), and *The Subterraneans* (1960, with Leslie Caron), his first major role.

That was closely followed by *Breakfast at Tiffany's* (1961), in which he played the lead opposite Audrey Hepburn. This was the role that propelled George Peppard to stardom and name-recognition status, if not to the pinnacle of celebrity status to which he may have aspired. Among his many ensuing movies were *How the West Was Won* (1962), *The Carpetbaggers* (1964), *Operation Crossbow* (1965), *Newman's Law* (1974), *Damnation Alley* (1977), and *Night of the Fox* (1990). In addition, Peppard directed and acted in *Five Days from Home* (1978).

On television he appeared in, among many other shows, *Studio One* and *Alfred Hitchcock Presents,* and he starred in *Banacek* (1972–74). When the *A-Team* opportunity came along in 1983, the by-now pragmatic actor was pleased to accept the team-leader's role that kept him working steadily for the next five years.

Divorced from Davies in 1964, he married (and divorced) actress Elizabeth Ashley twice. He married Laura Taylor in 1992, the same year he was diagnosed with lung cancer and finally gave up his two-pack-a-day habit. George Peppard had three children. He enjoyed regular exercising, sailing, hunting (for food only), reading, and writing until his 1994 passing.

Lee Powell

The first actor to play the Lone Ranger in the serial films that started in 1938, Lee Powell became a professional actor soon after graduating from college. Perhaps because he grew up so close to Hollywood, he was able to observe clearly that by following certain steps, he would become an actor. He trained at the Pasadena Playhouse, signed with Republic Pictures through a talent scout, and, by the time his country got into World War II, Lee Powell had become an established actor.

Married (to Norma R. Powell), with a daughter, and at age thirty-three, Powell easily could have avoided military service. Instead, the Lone Ranger elected to do what he saw as his duty to his country: he enlisted in the Marine Corps, where he would remain for the rest of his all-too-brief life.

(Photofest)

Born in Long Beach on 15 May 1908, Lee Berrien Powell was a track and football star at Long Beach Junior College and then at the University of Montana. After appearing in a few movies, such as *Forlorn River* and *The Last Gangster* (both 1937), he was cast in *The Lone Ranger*. This film series was produced as a result of the tremendous popularity of the radio program, which Americans listened to the same way we watch television these days: to forget daily problems while immersing ourselves in tales of adventure and mystery. Other favorite shows included *Ma Perkins, Just Plain Bill, Stella Dallas,* and *Jack Armstrong, the All-American Boy.*

The *Lone Ranger* was first broadcast in January 1933 over station WXYZ, Detroit. Several radio actors played the mystery champion of the downtrodden, a hero who became so beloved that by 1938, the first *Lone Ranger* movie was made. Lee Powell starred in all fifteen episodes of the first series, sometimes also called *Hi-Yo Silver*. In 1939 a second series, *The Lone Ranger Rides Again,* was made, also in fifteen episodes. This time actor Robert Livingston played the masked rider.

Before enlisting in the Marines, Powell was also cast in several other Westerns and serial films, including *Fighting Devil Dogs* (1938; Powell played a Marine), *The Return of Daniel Boone* (1941), and *Along the Sundown Trail* (1942). He enlisted on 17 August 1942 and was ordered to the 7th Recruit Battalion, Recruit Depot, San Diego.

After completing boot camp, he was ordered to Headquarters Company, 2d Battalion, 18th Marines (Engineers), 2d Marine Division, at Camp Elliott, California. In November 1942 he shipped out aboard the SS *President Monroe* at San Diego, bound for Wellington, New Zealand. Powell was with the 2d Marine Division when it invaded Saipan on 15 June 1944. Living through that, on 26 July he landed on the island of Tinian, which he helped capture in a ferocious battle that lasted until 30 July.

Tinian represented a significant victory for the American forces, since it provided an airfield from which US B-29 Superfortresses could operate against the home islands of Japan. The aircraft that dropped atomic bombs on Hiroshima and Nagasaki flew out of Tinian.

Sgt. Lee Powell lived through some of the bloodiest battles of the Pacific War. But then, on the same day that the Tinian battle ended, he

Upon sighting the enemy, Marines mopping up Tinian island drop into firing position, 2 August 1944.

died of acute poisoning. Newspapers at the time assumed he had been killed in action, but Sergeant Powell's USMC files report not only the alcohol poisoning, but some sort of "misconduct," the nature of which was "undetermined." Hypothetically, it must have had something to do with cutting loose a bit too much after having survived the hellish battles in which he was involved, perhaps by celebrating with vast quantities of methyl alcohol. Even small amounts of this highly toxic substance can kill; it can only be hoped that the courageous and successful warrior at least got to have one last good party with his buddies.

But the United States's erstwhile masked man carried the mystery to his grave. He was buried in the Marine Cemetery on Tinian and later, at the request of his father, moved to the National Cemetery of the Pacific in Honolulu.

Sergeant Powell, age thirty-five when he died, was posthumously awarded the Purple Heart, the Asiatic-Pacific Area Campaign Medal with two stars, and the Victory Medal World War II. The latter two awards were sent to his widow in September 1948.

Camp Elliott

Situated in California on the Kearney Mesa, just above the Mexican border and northeast of San Diego in the Sierra Madre mountains, Camp Elliott served as the point of embarkation for thousands of Marines who were bound for the South and Central Pacific combat zones during World War II. The area had been used for military purposes long before World War II, ever since the mesa had been named after an American general who had fought against Mexico for control of California. It was so vast that it also accommodated naval and Marine auxiliary air station Camp Kearney, the Marine Corps air depot Camp Miramar, and the Marine Corps rifle range Camp Matthews.

The Marine Corps began using large portions of it between 1934 and 1942, when the city of San Diego leased to the Corps about 363 acres of land on the Kearney Mesa, to be used mostly for machine-gun and artillery practice and unit training. When President Franklin Delano Roosevelt declared a limited national emergency on 8 September 1939, temporary buildings were erected on the mesa; by June 1940, the section that had previously been named Camp Holcomb was renamed, in honor of former Marine Corps commandant Maj. Gen. George F. Elliott.

An unlimited national emergency was announced on 27 May 1941, with the attendant expansion of all U.S. armed forces. There was an immediate requirement for more Marine Corps training space near San Diego, and between 1941 and 1942, 28,879 more acres of land were acquired. In April 1942, the Training Center at Camp Elliott was officially activated, and during 1942, most Corps activities took place there. Camp Elliott, which comprised several former farms, including Green Farm and Jacques Farm, covered 32,000 acres. The hilly, rugged terrain was ideally suited to advanced training of troops after boot camp, most of whom spent eight to ten weeks there before being shipped out from the city docks.

Scattered around, the training facilities and equipment included three permanent subsidiary camps, four bivouac areas, and forty-one combat or firing ranges. Nearly thirty schools in the Training Center offered a widely varied curriculum, which included infantry schooling, specialist schools, the Marine Corps's only tank school (at Jacques Farm), a parachute-training school, a scout and sniper school, and an officer candidate detachment (at Green Farm). Also attached to the School Battalion were the Japanese Language School, Motor Transport School, Quartermaster School, and Shoe and Textile Repair School. At Linda Vista, a final tune-up camp readied replacement battalions who were scheduled to be shipped overseas.

Camp Elliott was deactivated in 1947, following the end of World War II.

Tyrone Power

This megastar of the late 1930s and 1940s, a man of such physical attractiveness that catching a glimpse of it in a mirror must at times have surprised even himself, started out on 5 May 1914, when he was born in Cincinnati, Ohio. His great-grandfather, William Grattan Tyrone Power, had been a famous Irish actor, and his parents, Frederick Tyrone and Helen Power (better known by their stage names of Tyrone Power and Patia Réaume), were Shakespearean actors. His father worked on the stage and in silent movies in New York and Hollywood, but his preference for traveling solo did the marriage no good, and shortly after the birth of their second child, Anne, the Powers were divorced.

The family had in the meantime moved to California, where Patia found acting work on the stage, entrusting her children to the care of a nanny. When she was at home, she worked with the children on their own beginning acting lessons, teaching them techniques for breathing and projecting their voices. Tyrone Edmund put this early training to good use at age seven, when he appeared onstage for the first time and successfully delivered his one line.

Young Tyrone may not have paid for those lessons, but the value of a dollar was instilled in him back in Cincinnati, where Patia returned with the children in 1922, having emerged from a second divorce. While attending various Catholic schools, Tyrone worked as a drugstore soda-jerk and as an usher at the nearby movie theater. Predictably, he was fascinated with all things theater related, and as he grew older he began to find work on the stage in minor roles. By age sixteen his aspiration was to become a star. Tyrone Sr. encouraged and nourished this hope through his letters to "Bingo," as he called his son.

In 1931, after his graduation from Purcell High School, Bingo joined his father in Canada, where the two spent almost two months fishing, talking about theater, getting to know each other. They then went on to Chicago, where Senior appeared as Shylock in *The Merchant of Venice* while Junior played an extra. Next Senior was offered work in Hollywood, and the twosome went out to the coast. After several supporting roles, Tyrone Sr. was offered a more meaty part in the movie *The Miracle Man* (1932). But it was work he would never get to do—Frederick Tyrone collapsed of a heart attack in his son's arms in late 1931, as the two were preparing to go out with friends for the evening. *The Big Trail* (1930), his first talkie, was his last film.

Tyrone Jr. who had been unsuccessfully seeking work, stayed on in Hollywood after his father's death, carrying on the family tradition. But it was the Great Depression, and work was not easily found. After much trial and error, a few mild successes, and a stint in Chicago working in radio and at the World's Fair in 1933 and again in 1934, he found steady acting work with a Chicago stock company. In time, through friends, this took him to New York, where he was introduced to everyone his friends could think of.

Producer and director Guthrie McClintic and his wife, actress Katharine Cornell, were among those to whom the handsome young actor was presented as if he were some rare object. But charming

Tyrone knew how to make good conversation, and, what was more, he was sincere. His earnest, fine manner and trusting nature won over everyone he met.

The McClintics represented a definite start. Power's work with their company took him around the country, including to Los Angeles. Power had been taking fencing and French lessons, applying himself assiduously to improving his performances, and he was noticed. Then, back in New York, his interpretation of Benvolio in *Romeo and Juliet* attracted the attention of both coasts. This was followed by a more high-profile role in George Bernard Shaw's *Saint Joan,* which the company took on the road. In Los Angeles a scout from Twentieth-Century Fox offered Power a seven-year contract, which he accepted.

By this time Patia and Anne had moved to California as well, and the family found itself reunited. Despite his already substantial beginnings in acting, Power was thoroughly groomed by studio head Darryl Francis Zanuck, who guarded the actor jealously, rarely loaning him out to other studios for the duration of his first contract (he would sign a second one in 1945). He and wife Annabella did manage to squeeze in a play in 1941, *Liliom,* which drew unanimous cheers. Power starred in almost fifty films during his lifetime, most of them for Fox.

His first screen triumph was *Lloyds of London* (1936). His other notable preservice efforts included *Café Metropole* (1937), *Alexander's Ragtime Band* (1938), *Rose of Washington Square* (1939), *Jesse James* (1939), *A Yank in the R.A.F.* (1941), *Blood and Sand* (1941), *This Above All* (1942), and *The Black Swan* (1942). By the time he entered the service, Tyrone Power was a favorite with movie fans.

In 1939 he married the French actress Annabella, born Suzanne Charpentier in Paris. Their marriage lasted until 1948, despite Power's well-known trysts and affairs. He was the constant object of romantic (and lustful) attentions, which he did not always resist. His unquestioned professional integrity and genuinely caring nature made him all the more irresistible, and Tyrone Power was loved by everyone who knew him. It was impossible to dislike this man, who managed to remain on good terms with Annabella even after their divorce.

On 3 September 1939, Tyrone and Annabella were on their way

back to the States after a European honeymoon. Their plane was refueling when they heard that England and France had declared war against Germany. Several weeks later Annabella returned to by-now perilous France, bringing her daughter back to California with her. (Tyrone would officially adopt Annie before leaving for the Pacific with the Marines.) Annabella's parents preferred to remain in France—though farther away from Paris—and she made fruitless attempts to convince her teenage brother, who could not get a passport, to be smuggled out. In early 1944 Vichy France would summon Pierre Charpentier to military service, which he avoided by disappearing into the countryside for several days. But the exposure led to his death anyway.

Annabella had no way of knowing what was in store for Pierre, and, having done all she could, she could only hope for her family's survival. Back in Hollywood, the Powers hosted Sunday get-togethers attended by their numerous famous neighbors. In early 1941 Zanuck made a film about Britain's ongoing air war, *A Yank in the R.A.F.*, casting Power as the lead. Released later that year, it was a great commercial success, and Zanuck agreed to the Powers' going off to Connecticut to work together in *Liliom*. By December 1941 they were back in Hollywood to receive the dreadful news of Pearl Harbor.

Zanuck threw himself into the fray immediately, volunteering his services. In a jiffy he was made a lieutenant colonel in the Army, ordered to England to oversee training films. Displeased with this cushy assignment, the studio head received permission to participate in the Northern African invasion, filming the Allied operations. He was promoted to colonel in 1942.

Tyrone enlisted in the Naval Reserve in April 1942, with prospects of being a chief petty officer assigned to a morale and recreational activity. While awaiting his call to active duty, he patrolled on air-raid watch twice a week. All along the United States's coastlines, watches had been set up to guard against possible enemy attack or infiltration. That summer he and Annabella hosted a well-attended sale on the grounds of their estate, Saltair. Their rich and famous friends donated personal possessions and their time, and together they raised money for the Free French Relief Committee. Tyrone continued to make movies, increasingly disturbed about the Japanese forces' progress in the Pacific.

In the spring Annabella had toured the country starring in the play

Blithe Spirit, the name that her husband would later pick for his Marine transport aircraft. By July, as Tyrone was making *Crash Dive* (1943), he became worried that the studio could be slowing production on the film to keep him working and out of the war. He promptly went to the Navy recruiting station to check on his active-duty status, but no record of him could be found. An angry Tyrone Power then tried to offer his services as a pilot, but he was declared unqualified and informed that he could enlist in the Navy only as an ordinary seaman. This would not do, and furthermore, Power resolved not to renew any efforts to entertain for the service.

Meanwhile, the Marines were landing on the Solomon Islands and beginning the savage battle for Guadalcanal. As Power listened to radio broadcasts about Marine air support bombing pathways for Leathernecks on the ground, he decided that was where he belonged: he already held a pilot's license (his open-cockpit plane awaited him in a hangar in New Mexico).

On 24 August 1942 he enlisted in the U.S. Marine Corps in San Diego. He was ordered to active duty in January 1943, and he underwent boot-camp training at Camp Elliot, San Diego. At the end of his training he was named the "honor man" of his platoon and had earned badges for both sharpshooting and marksmanship. He wore these with great pride.

Power was one of seventy-two recruits selected for Officer Candidate School after graduating from boot training. He completed OCS at Quantico, Virginia, on 2 June 1943, and was commissioned a reserve second lieutenant. Bent on becoming a flying Leatherneck, he applied and was accepted for flight training, and was ordered to Naval Air Station, Corpus Christi, Texas, for instruction. There he also sometimes served as officer of the day (OOD); Marines who were "on post," walking along the sea wall in the middle of the chilly night, later recalled that Power was the only OOD who would bring them a thermos of hot coffee.

While Tyrone was completing his Marine training, Annabella had joined a tour selling war bonds. She spent several weeks with her husband in Corpus Christi after the strenuous schedule had exhausted her forces. She needed abundant rest, which she was able to get while Tyrone trained all day and she stayed in the hotel suite he'd retained for getaways from military rigors. The Powers were determined to save their marriage if they could, though Annabella was tiring of Tyrone's apparent inability to cease his wandering ways. Meanwhile she continued her work, appearing onstage and drawing consistent critical accolades.

On 13 April 1944, Tyrone received his naval aviator wings and was promoted to first lieutenant. Next he was ordered to Naval Air Station Atlanta for instrument flight instruction, after which he joined Marine Transport Squadron 352, 9th Marine Air Wing, Fleet Marine Forces (FMF). He flew twin-engine R4Ds—also known as Dakotas—serving with the squadron at Marine Corps Air Stations Cherry Point (North Carolina) and El Centro (California), the latter one of the West Coast jumping-off points for Marines going to the Pacific.

When Paris was liberated in August 1944, Annabella, anxious to see her family again, joined the USO, cast as the star of the play *Blithe Spirit*. Soon the troupe headed for Europe. While entertaining in Italy, Annabella was cleared to fly aboard a military aircraft going to Paris, where she finally was reunited with her family. She spent a few weeks with them before catching up with her *Blithe Spirit* company, which itself was unsuccessfully chasing General Patton's Third Army as it sped through France toward the German border.

Tyrone Power finally went to war in March 1945. He was ordered to join Marine Transport Squadron 353, Marine Air Group 21, 4th Marine Air Wing. The squadron was equipped with C-46 Curtiss Commando transport aircraft and stationed on the island of Saipan, which had been retaken from the Japanese in June 1944. Power flew in supplies and carried out casualties from Iwo Jima and Okinawa. He was one of the pilots who helped to evacuate the wounded from Yontan Airstrip, Okinawa, while it was still under fire.

He got through the war unscathed, despite the antiaircraft fire he drew whenever he flew near the front. The *Blithe Spirit*'s ailerons caused a little trouble on one occasion, when they refused to do their job shortly after takeoff, but they were unlocked after maneuvering over the airfield.

Entertainment groups visited Saipan while Power was stationed there, and stars such as Gertrude Lawrence arrived on the base as members of ENSA—Entertainments National Services Association, the British equivalent of the USO. It soon became apparent to Power that

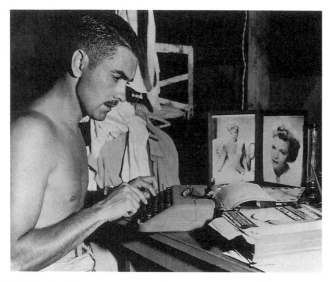

While in the Pacific, Power wrote his impressions of the war's devastation to friends and family. (On his desk are photos of wife Annabella).

Marine 1st Lt. Tyrone Power takes time out at the Omura Naval Air Station, Kyushu, Japan, to sweat out the chow line and get himself a cup of "Jo."

Navy chief photographer's mate Leif Erickson, another Hollywood émigré, met with Marine 1st Lt. Tyrone Power at Yontan airfield, Okinawa, April 1945.

the island did not have adequate stage facilities to offer these groups, and he set about designing and helping oversee the construction of an outdoor stage, called the Roosevelt Memorial Theater in honor of the late president. It opened the first week of June 1945 to the swinging sounds of Dick Jergens and his Marine band. Before joining the Corps, Jergens had been a popular dance-band leader and recording artist.

Power also managed movie showings for his fellow Marines' regular entertainment. He imposed on these presentations the same expectations he had of himself in Hollywood and onstage. He screened films each morning and made sure the projectors were shipshape; he expected professional-level film splicing. Everything had to be done the right way in Tyrone Power's wartime movie theater.

When the United States dropped the atomic bomb on Hiroshima

Power's squadron flew C-46 Curtiss Commando transport planes on supply and casualty missions to and from Iwo Jima and Okinawa.

on 6 August 1945, for all practical purposes the war was over. Tyrone Power was one of those who flew to Japan bringing supplies to the Marine troops occupying the country. He was appalled by the devastation the bomb had wreaked, writing to a friend that not only had the world changed forever, it probably would be destroyed as a result of this horrifying new weapon. While flying to and from Japan with various cargo, he took advantage of an opportunity to join a few others for a jeep ride to Yokohama, near Tokyo. Wherever he went he observed a defeated but proud, resentful people whose country was in ruins.

By November, Power was on Guam awaiting orders and transportation home. He found passage on the USS *Marvin H. McIntyre* (APA-129), which was sailing for Portland, Oregon. The ship arrived on 21 November 1945, and he was surprised to see Annabella at dockside. Once the ship was tied down, Power jumped over the railing of the vessel and, cheered by several hundred Marines, ran to the embrace of his wife. Annabella had assembled the surviving family at Saltair, where the household now included her mother (her father had died earlier that year) and daughter, as well as Tyrone's sister and niece. Patia was nearby but preferred to live in her own apartment.

Power was discharged from active duty on 15 January 1946, assigned to the 11th Marine Corps Reserve District, Los Angeles. He reached the rank of captain in May 1951, and major in 1957. For his wartime service, Tyrone Power was awarded the American Campaign Medal, the Asiatic-Pacific Area Campaign Medal with one bronze star, the World War II Victory Medal, and the Navy Occupation Service Medal with Asia clasp. He maintained his reserve status for the rest of his life, and he went out of his way to greet Marines whenever he encountered them.

Returning to Fox, he starred in Somerset Maugham's *The Razor's Edge* (1946), to mixed critical reviews. Other films followed, proving that the sparkle of his star had not dimmed while he was away. *Nightmare Alley* appeared in 1947, and *Captain from Castile* (1947) became one of Fox's major postwar successes. Although Power's films of the late 1940s and 1950s received few cheers from film critics, he was still a strong presence on the screen, and fans continued to flock to his films. In 1957 he gave three of his best performances in *Abandon Ship, The Sun Also Rises,* and *Witness for the Prosecution.* He appeared on the stage in 1950 in the lead role of a London presentation of *Mister Roberts,* which won him reviewers' praise.

Unlike his career, his marriage declined irreparably after the initial elation of reunion had worn off. He and Annabella remained close, but it became clear to both that true intimacy between them could not be recovered.

Tyrone Power died in 1958 in Madrid, at age forty-four. While making the movie *Solomon and Sheba* the actor, who had been smoking and drinking too much, working too hard, and generally taking poor care of himself, suffered a fatal heart attack. His wife accompanied his remains aboard a Trans World Airlines aircraft sent by controlling shareholder Howard Hughes. The plane carried Power back to California, where he was buried in Hollywood Memorial Park.

As a U.S. Marine Corps veteran of World War II, Maj. Tyrone Power was accorded full military honors. His six pallbearers were Marine Corps officers with whom he had served in the war, and the

Marine Honor Guard from El Toro Marine Air Station, Santa Ana, rendered military honors during the burial ceremony.

He had married twice more after his divorce from Annabella, first to actress Linda Christian (1949–56, producing daughters Romina Francesca and Taryn, who would later briefly become actresses), and then to Deborah Ann Minardos (1958). When she lost her husband, Deborah was carrying Tyrone Power, Jr., another actor, whom his father would have liked to know and who was born in 1959.

John Russell

T his Western enthusiast was known for being just as upstanding and law-abiding in real life as was the character he portrayed on television from 1958 to 1962, Marshal Dan Troop, the *Lawman*. His father, U.S. Naval Academy graduate John Henry Russell, had survived the sinking of the cruiser *San Diego* in 1918, when it struck a mine in the Long Island Sound. Had he not, John would never have been born on 8 January 1921 in Los Angeles, one of five children whom John Henry and his wife raised with an acute awareness and pride of their California-pioneer ancestry. The younger John went on to attend the University of California, where he studied drama.

He tried twice to join the Marines before the Japanese attack on Pearl Harbor, but he was turned down because he towered above the rest of the Marines, at his six feet, four inches—too tall, until the standards were eased in 1942. While waiting for a hoped-for waiver on his

(Photofest)

application, he remained in Southern California and worked at Inter-state Aircraft. There he did everything from helping mechanics to sweeping the floor, and eventually he worked his way up to material-control chief. Finally, on 10 February 1942, John Russell was signed up in the Corps.

He reported to the Marine Corps Recruit Depot, San Diego, for seven weeks of boot camp, two of them at the rifle range. After com-pleting his initial training, he was transferred to Camp Elliot and selected as an officer candidate. John Russell was commissioned a sec-ond lieutenant, USMC, on 11 November 1942.

Assigned to the 6th Marine Regiment, 2d Marine Division, Lieu-tenant Russell boarded a ship bound for Wellington, Noumea, and the Solomon Islands. His unit was ordered to reinforce the battle-hard-ened Marines of the 1st Division on Guadalcanal.

The first U.S. offensive of the war against the Japanese had recently taken place on this South Pacific island in the Solomon chain. The invasion had been planned to counter Japanese advances in the area that had been directed toward Australia. The Marines had landed on Guadalcanal on 7 August 1942, but six months would pass before the last Japanese soldier was defeated. Of the 60,000 Americans in the campaign, 1,600 were killed, with another 4,200 wounded. There had been about 36,000 Japanese on Guadalcanal; of these, 14,000 were killed, 900 died of disease, and another 1,000 were captured. Aside from these serious losses on both sides ashore, both suffered as well heavy sea and air casualties while supporting the operation.

Russell survived Guadalcanal, serving as an assistant intelligence officer. But his career with the Corps was short-lived, due to the seri-ous malaria that he contracted while on the island, complicated by "assorted" other medical problems. He was shipped back to San Diego naval hospital for treatment, where his diagnosis was not good: it was determined that his illness would probably recur. He was listed as unfit for combat duty, and John Russell received a medical discharge from the Marine Corps.

Back in Los Angeles and celebrating with his wife—they'd been married before he'd gone overseas—the tall, dark, handsome, and still youthful war veteran stood out from the crowd in a Beverly Hills restaurant. Soon, the talent scout who'd noticed him signed John Rus-

A young Marine shows John Russell some of the latest weaponry.

sell to a contract with Universal-International. He would also later have contracts with Twentieth-Century Fox, Republic, and Warner Brothers.

The dozens of films in which he was cast, usually as either a good- or a bad-guy heavyweight, include *A Bell for Adano* (1945), *Somewhere in the Night* (1946), *Sitting Pretty* (1948), *The Last Command* (1955), *Fort Massacre* (1958), *Rio Bravo* (1959), *Legacy of Blood* (1973), *The Outlaw Josey Wales* (1976, starring Clint Eastwood), *Six Tickets to Hell* (1976), *Honkytonk Man* (1982, with Eastwood), *Pale Rider* (1985, again with Eastwood; Russell played the villainous Marshal Stockburn), and *Under the Gun* (1986).

Russell also appeared in television series (such as *Cheyenne*, 1958), and he starred in *Soldiers of Fortune* (1955–56) and *Lawman*. The highly principled actor strongly identified with Marshal Troop, arising early each day to study his lines so that he could spend evenings in the company of his family (married and divorced twice, he had three children).

He loved the Western genre and the out-of-doors, and he enjoyed skeet shooting with fellow Hollywoodian Robert Stack, who'd been a gunnery training officer in the Navy. For the latter part of his life, Russell lived simply in an apartment in Hollywood, engrossed in the myriad books on his crammed shelves. A chain smoker, he suffered increasingly from the emphysema that would be his undoing.

Russell remained a Marine at heart, wearing with pride the ring of a fellow Corpsman killed in action in Vietnam; Lt. Col. Pat Murray, USMC, of the Judge Advocate General's office, presented the ring to him in 1972. He died in 1991 and was given a military funeral. John Russell is buried at Santelle Military Cemetery, Westwood, California.

Robert Ryan

A t age eight, Robert Bushnell Ryan lost his little brother to influenza. When he was twenty-six, his father died as a result of complications after being hit by a car. Socially active, prideful, Irish-descended Ryan wanted to do something useful during his own life, however short it might turn out to be. Married to one woman for life—actress-turned-writer Jessica Cadwalader—with three children to support, educate, and guide, Ryan not only worked steadily, he also made time for involvement in organizations such as the National Committee for a Sane Nuclear Policy (SANE) and the American Civil Liberties Union (ACLU). An active Democrat, he worked for better race relations and for disarmament. He helped to organize and direct a theater group at the University of California at Los Angeles, and in 1951, he and Jessica founded and helped direct the Oakwood School,

(Photofest)

with the mission of promoting humanistic values. The school, which opened in their backyard, is now considered one of the best in the country.

Ryan was born in Chicago on 11 November 1909, to Mabel and Timothy Ryan. His father was a prosperous builder whose fervent hope was that his firstborn would grow up to take over the business. But Robert, educated at Jesuit schools and rounded out with private lessons in violin and boxing, showed more of a penchant for literature and drama. By age eighteen he'd read Shakespeare, Chekhov, and Shaw, and he showed up regularly at the film studio in his neighborhood, the Essanay, hoping to be picked as an extra—which he was, for at least two silent films: 1927's *The College Widow* and 1929's *Strong Boy*.

At Dartmouth College in New Hampshire (1927), Ryan wrote articles for the campus newspaper and joined the fight against Prohibition. He also played football, ran track, and won the heavyweight boxing title in his freshman year. He retained the title throughout all four of his years at Dartmouth.

The six-foot-four, wavy-haired, brown-eyed, powerful college graduate (English Literature, 1931) then went out into the world in search of a reporting job. This failed to materialize, and Ryan went to work instead in the engine room of a freighter shipping out from Brooklyn for Africa. His two-year job taught him how to stoke coal, clean bilges, and suffer through rough seas. He'd had just about enough of it all by the time he got back to New York, where the news of his father's accident awaited him.

Ryan went straight home to help out with the family business while his father recuperated. This experience convinced him that he would most definitely *not* be taking over the business. As soon as the father could take over again, the son was off in search of what his true calling might be. He tried panning for gold and being a cowboy in Montana. But then Timothy Ryan passed away and Robert again rushed home.

After helping Mabel through the shock, arrangements, and aftermath, Robert stayed in Chicago and worked at a variety of jobs, including modeling clothing in a department store, bodyguarding, selling graveyard plots, and collecting bills. He especially disliked the latter position, which inevitably involved getting money from people who did not have it, and he soon quit. Meanwhile, acting had again attracted his notice. He'd acted in an amateur play through someone he'd met at the department store and parlayed his way into directing a production at a girls' school. Finally he signed up for some lessons given by a retired stock-company actor. He enjoyed them so much that he moved to Hollywood, after a small investment in oil drilling paid unexpectedly handsome returns. Three hundred dollars turned into two thousand, allowing him both to provide for his mother and to relocate to where he could attend the Pasadena Playhouse.

But he arrived in California too late: that season's classes had already begun. Someone suggested that he try instead Max Reinhardt's Actor's Workshop. It was to be the beginning of a successful and rewarding career, and it also introduced him to Jessica, a tall, dark-haired beauty who was a fellow acting student. She became his wife in 1939, well before graduation day.

Following Reinhardt's course, Ryan auditioned and was selected for a part in the play *Too Many Husbands,* written by Somerset Maugham. That led to a contract with Paramount and his first film, *Golden Gloves* (1940), which led to a few other minor efforts. But his contract was not renewed the next year (nor was Susan Hayward's).

So Robert and Jessica Ryan went east and worked on the stage, Jessica supplementing with modeling and working on her writing. She eventually would publish many articles as well as several books. A role in the play *Clash by Night* attracted the favorable attention of critics, as well as that of an RKO Radio Pictures talent scout. Before long the Ryans were on their way back to Hollywood, armed with Robert's brand new six-hundred-dollar-a-week contract.

This time, success stuck. Robert Ryan made seven films in two years, ever improving as an actor. He met and befriended Pat O'Brien, who championed him and got him cast (with O'Brien) in *The Iron Major* (1943). The male lead in *Tender Comrade* (1943) soon followed, opposite Ginger Rogers, after which Ryan's future as an actor was guaranteed. *Marine Raiders* (1944) came next, with Pat O'Brien, and then came the real Marines.

Robert Ryan enlisted in the U.S. Marine Corps in January 1944. He was trained as a drill instructor, assigned to Camp Pendleton. The

During filming of *Marine Raiders* at Camp Elliott, former Dartmouth undefeated heavyweight champ Ryan compares notes with former Western Intercollegiate Boxing champ Maj. Carl V. Larsen, USMC. (Radio Pictures, Photofest)

extremely creative Marine took up abstract painting during his time at the Southern California barracks, producing a hellish self-portrait. It may have been a way for him to grapple with the inner battle stirred up by having to play the real-life role of a tough, no-nonsense Marine trainer, all the while knowing that many of these fresh-faced boys would never survive the war.

Ryan was equally affected by many of the war veterans who did return. He watched as the wounded and crippled tried to cope with uncertain futures. He saw the horror behind the haunted gaze of those who had lived through unimaginable conditions, leaving comrades forever behind.

He found his impressions reflected in a book that he read around this time: future director and screenwriter Richard Brooks's *The Brick Foxhole* (Harper, 1945). The novel's subject was the effects of war on returning veterans, and Ryan was so moved by it that he asked the author, a fellow Marine whom he met at Pendleton, to keep him in mind for the lead role, should the book ever become a movie. It later did, and Ryan won a best-supporting-actor Academy Award nomination for his interpretation of a bigot in the controversial film-noir classic *Crossfire,* which won best social film at the 1947 Cannes Film Festival.

Private First Class Ryan was discharged in November 1945, by which time he was a committed pacifist, a position that Jessica, a Quaker, encouraged. Unlike most other actors, Ryan was in the enviable position of having been assured that RKO would still consider him under contract after his military service had been completed. Thus, even though it was a while before he was again cast in a picture, he could rely on a steady income.

By 1947 his film career was back on track. Before its end, the many films to which Robert Ryan contributed his impressive talent included *Berlin Express* (1948), *The Set-Up* (1949), *Bad Day at Black Rock* (1955), *God's Little Acre* (1958), *Billy Budd* (1962), *The Dirty Dozen* (1967), *The Wild Bunch* (1969), *The Love Machine* (1971), and *The Iceman Cometh* (1973). He also enjoyed success on television and the stage, preferring the theater to all of his other performing endeavors.

The Ryans kept homes in New York and North Hollywood, with plenty of room for children and pets. Robert died in 1973, a year after losing Jessica.

George C. Scott

George Campbell Scott has been feisty practically since his 18 October 1927 birth in Wise, Virginia, where his father, George D., worked as a coal-mine surveyor. The Great Depression shut down that operation, and George D. moved the family to Pontiac, Michigan, for his new job at the Buick assembly plant. He worked long hours—eventually he would rise to the position of vice president of Ex-Cell-O Corp., Detroit. His wife, Helen, held down the fort at home. She also wrote poetry, gave readings, and taught her two children to enjoy reading stories aloud. But that early training in elocution ended all too soon, when Helen succumbed to peritonitis. George D. remarried four years later.

The loss of his mother was overwhelming for eight-year-old George, whose outrage turned to violence in football games and any other physical activity that he could attack. Helped by his older sister, he managed to stay alive long enough for his mother's influence to burgeon into artistic expression. He began to write, an avocation that he would continue until he turned his creative energies to acting.

At Redford High School in Detroit, the six-foot, robust Scott focused on baseball. He enlisted in the Marines (16 June 1945) after graduating, ready and able to fight. He was ordered in early August 1945 to report to Parris Island for boot training. But by the time he had finished in boot class Platoon 329, the war was over.

After Parris Island he was sent to Washington, D.C., to Marine Barracks, the Corps's oldest post (established 1801) and residence of the commandant since 1805. Scott was assigned to the Marine Corps Institute, housed at the Barracks as the Corps's correspondence school since 1920.

Marines attached to Washington's Marine Barracks were tasked— and still are today—with a variety of mostly public-relations duties, including performing at parades and ceremonies and giving public concerts. The Marine Band, based at the Barracks since 1801 and led by John Philip Sousa from 1880 to 1892, is probably the most famous of the service bands. Other duties included providing White House security details, acting as escorts for presidential society functions, providing color guard units for special occasions, and serving as part of the grave detail during military honors for veterans buried at the Arlington National Cemetery.

Scott's duties included grave detail at Arlington. Previously disappointed about missing out on real-live combat, after watching hundreds of burials and veiled, devastated widows, Scott began to see war in the more brutal light of reality. He and his pals commiserated about it all over drinks in a bar (and sometimes even before they got off work), where Scott would sometimes get riled up and get into a brawl. His violent temper—witness his broken nose—would get both himself and others into trouble over the years, and it was in the service that he began his long, on-again, off-again battle to control his tendency to quaff far too much alcohol.

Discharged as a staff sergeant on 15 June 1949, Scott received the World War II Victory Medal and the Good Conduct Medal. He used the GI Bill to attend the University of Missouri. Scott was twenty-one

Scott stands in upper right corner of this August 1945 shot of Platoon 329, Parris Island.

years old and already fighting his own private war, in which his excessive drinking habit fought for control over his life. But inner turbulence did not keep him from finding his path, nor from working to realize it. While at Missouri, he noticed a call for auditions for the Missouri Workshop's production of the play *The Winslow Boy*.

Winning the lead part (he'd memorized the whole play), Scott knew immediately that this was the thing for him. Everything seemed to click, fall into place. He instinctively knew what to do. For George C. Scott, this had to be it. He studied drama (and journalism) and worked with the theater group for the next four years, performing in university productions.

He then moved to the drama department of women's Stephens College, Columbia, Missouri, where he taught a literature course and continued to develop his acting skills, appearing nearly continuously in the school's many plays. The intense, passionate teacher/actor of the one-sided smile was extremely popular with his students, one of whom, Carolyn Hughes, he married in 1951.

The Scotts moved on to a small Detroit stock company, where George supplemented his paltry paycheck with various construction jobs. He tried to make his marriage work (it didn't; they were divorced in 1954), then moved to Washington, D.C. There he worked for his brother-in-law's construction company and gave up acting for a while. But it nagged at him, and finally he joined another troupe, working on construction jobs by day and on stage by night.

He married actress Patricia Reed in 1954, and the Scotts moved to New York. Pat worked as a secretary and George in a bank, nights, so he could go on auditions during the days. All the while, from rejection to depressing rejection, he fought his attraction toward self-annihilation. Finally, in 1957 he landed the lead role in *Richard III* for the New York Shakespeare Festival. It was the start of a great actor's brilliant career.

He went on to act in the plays *As You Like It* and *Children of Darkness,* then movies, starting with *The Hanging Tree* (1959). His second film effort, *Anatomy of a Murder* (1959), won him his first supporting-actor Academy Award nomination; later, he would try to reject them. Since those early days, the many vehicles through which George C. Scott has terrified or otherwise thoroughly entertained his audiences have included *Dr. Strangelove: Or How I Learned to Stop Worrying and Love the Bomb* (1964; as stomach-slapping Gen. Buck Turgidson, who tussled on the war-room floor with the Russian ambassador as the world ended), *Petulia* (1968), *Jane Eyre* (1971), *Islands in the Stream* (1977), *Taps* (1981), *The Exorcist III* (1990), and *Malice* (1993).

He narrated the documentary *The Indomitable Teddy Roosevelt* (1984) and directed the films *Rage* (1972) and *The Savage Is Loose* (1974). Since the 1980s he has worked increasingly in television, notably in the films *Oliver Twist* (1982, he played Fagin) and *A Christmas Carol* (1984, as Scrooge), and in the miniseries *Mussolini: The Untold Story* (1985, as Il Duce). His television work has also included appearances on *Kraft Theatre, Dow Hour of Great Mysteries, Playhouse 90, Hallmark Hall of Fame, Ben Casey, The Virginian,* and the bold, realistic series *East Side, West Side* (1963–64), in which he starred, and which won a National Critics Award and several Emmy nominations.

A dedicated perfectionist, Scott has always preferred the theater, where he's appeared repeatedly on Broadway and in the New York Shakespeare Festival, garnering several Obie awards along the way. He took on the Academy of Motion Picture Arts and Sciences by refusing to accept a best-actor Academy Award (1970, for *Patton*), after already having tried to reject a prior nomination for his supporting role in *The Hustler* (1961; he was informed that one could reject an award itself, but not a nomination). Scott felt that the celebrity fest had nothing to do with the profession of acting, which he saw in the more traditional sense of theater as part of real people's lives, in real communities.

He put his money where is mouth was. Scott was interested not just in complaining about how the original raison d'être of the performing arts was being gobbled up by Hollywood, then regurgitated in ready-to-eat, glitzy packages. He wanted authentic, for-the-people, by-the-people theater, something in which Americans could become as involved as they were in baseball.

In the early 1960s, he tried to set up the first of a nationwide group of regional theaters in which resident companies could perform and hone their craft, taking the best of their work to Broadway. Here, too, younger actors could study and develop their skills, and New York would no longer dominate the world of theater in the United States. But the first two plays produced by Scott's Theatre of Michigan (formed in 1962, based in Detroit), *General Seeger* and *Great Day in the Morning,* bombed on Broadway. Scott, refusing to allow the corporation to declare bankruptcy, insisted on paying off the debt himself, over the next several years.

Powerful and furious, charismatic and compassionate, with a sweeping sense of humor, George C. Scott has not done anything in a small way. After being divorced from Pat in 1960, he was married three times more: to actress Colleen Dewhurst twice, 1960–65 and 1967–72; and to actress Trish Van Devere in 1972. He has five children, including two actors. This reckless, tempestuous champion of carefully selected causes is a private man who has consistently eluded bright lights and see-and-be-seen places and events, preferring to spend the time with his family. Aside from the stage and his literary interests, he's found pleasure in playing bridge, chess, golf, and softball, and in following baseball.

Tad Van Brunt

Frederick Baskerville Van Brunt was born in Yokohama, Japan, on 22 July 1921. It was his father, Dutch-American H. B., who began calling him Tad, after the son of his hero, Abraham Lincoln. As a buyer for major import-export companies in Japan, the elder Van Brunt immersed himself—and his British-descended wife and their four children—in the local culture, with its distinctive customs and traditions.

After the great earthquake of 1923, they relocated to Kobe, where Tad spent most of his childhood. With other foreign students, he attended the Canadian Academy, which did not keep him from becoming fluent in the country's native language. His playmates were largely Japanese, and his familiarity with their way of life earned him a respect that would endure the test of time, long after he had left Japan.

In 1939 the Van Brunts moved to Ontario, California, not far from

Los Angeles. Tad adjusted easily to the life of an American teenager, enjoying in particular his drama and theater classes at Chaffey High School. He appeared in numerous plays, and, after high-school grad-uation, he won a scholarship to the Pasadena Playhouse Drama School. By this time he had sprouted into a green-eyed, brown-haired six-footer, similar in looks to Clark Gable. He attended his new school for a year, but before his career could get under way, the United States got into World War II.

Tad joined the Navy, initially. Because he was fluent in Japanese and had a thorough understanding of Japan, both extremely rare and val-ued assets, he was sent to the Navy's Japanese-language school at the University of Colorado in Boulder, from where he graduated in July 1943. Students chose between the Navy and the Marines, and this time, Tad chose the Marines. He'd seen them as a boy, when he'd gone along with his dad on business trips to China. He'd been mesmerized by the cool attitude of the old Fourth Regiment Marines, the famous Horse Marines, as they paraded through the streets of Peiping.

Once in the Corps, Van Brunt went through further training at Camp Elliot's Jacques Farm. He then was sent to Guadalcanal, where he joined the 3d Division in preparing for the invasion to recapture Guam. Van Brunt became one of the Corps's best interrogators. Sit-ting with the Japanese prisoners of war, he found that thanks to his language ability and his understanding of them, they would talk to him. Thus Van Brunt was able to provide his superiors with a steady stream of valuable intelligence. During the course of his front-line activities, he was awarded a Bronze Star medal for capturing and dis-arming a high-ranking Japanese officer.

Next it was on to Okinawa. After ninety-three days of fierce fight-ing, the island fell to American forces on 2 July 1945. Marines of the 6th Marine Division, under the leadership of Maj. Gen. Lemuel C. Shepherd, USMC, played a major role in the defeat of the Japanese. One of Shepherd's staff members was Lt. Tad Van Brunt.

Van Brunt's reputation spread quickly among the native population, as he mingled with them, empathizing with their woes and helping out whenever he could. He allayed the terror of American cruelties that the Japanese had spread among them, tales so horrific that many civil-ians were found in the Okinawan caves along with Japanese soldiers.

On Okinawa, 1945, Van Brunt closely monitors the words of a prisoner asking his former comrades to surrender. In the background, another prisoner holds up a loudspeaker.

The Japanese had assured them that they would be tortured if they surrendered; many preferred to die in the caves with the Japanese soldiers, killed by American firepower, explosions, and flamethrowers. Some of the caves were sealed when the Japanese would not surrender.

Van Brunt convinced the Okinawans with whom he spoke that none of the horrors they had heard of were going to occur. On the contrary, he explained, Americans would bring them prosperity and technological advancement. (Nevertheless, today, Okinawans want the Marines to leave the island.)

Van Brunt soon began to receive Stateside notice for his Okinawan exploits, and an article about "the Fabulous Taisho" ran in the November 1945 issue of *Leatherneck*. The Okinawans, hearing of the

American who understood their language, culture, and problems, sought out Van Brunt to request his assistance in their dealings with the occupying government officials. They called him Taisho, or General. So popular did Taisho Van Brunt become that when it came time for him to leave them, the Okinawans petitioned Shepherd to let him stay on as the governor of their island. Their request appeared in *Leatherneck* magazine ("Return of the Taisho," February 1948):

> If, while the traditional culture of Okinawa still exists, it were impregnated with the seeds of your newer civilization, this land would become a new paradise of the Pacific; its people would be brought into contact with the blessings of your world, and would repay you with their everlasting gratitude. However, to effect this end, it is absolutely necessary that there be placed in charge, people who understand and sympathize with the Okinawans.
>
> We feel that Lieutenant Van Brunt, by virtue of his understanding of Okinawa, is the person best qualified to undertake the rebuilding of the country, a work in which men of such character must not be lacking.
>
> Please deign to allow this lieutenant to remain with us, to succour our people, condescend to let him assist in the construction of a New Okinawa under the American government.

However, there were military and civilian personnel who had been trained specifically to occupy enemy territory that had recently been taken: Van Brunt did not get the job. Instead of participating in the reconstruction and governing of Okinawa, he was sent with the 6th Marine Division to help repatriate Japanese soldiers of the Shantung Army in Tsingtao, China. There Van Brunt was assigned as a personal interpreter for the commander of the 3d Amphibious Corps, Maj. Gen. Keller E. Rockey.

Lieutenant Van Brunt was discharged from the Corps in early 1946. A well-connected friend had promised, back in 1941, to introduce him to a Paramount Studios executive when he got out. Van Brunt held him to his word, and a screen test led to a contract. This was followed by more acting classes and some bit parts.

The cheerful, well-liked former Marine followed the Hollywood path with aplomb, cracking jokes and patiently developing his craft.

Tad Van Brunt's acting career would never take him to great heights, but it did result in roles in *The Big Clock* (1948, starring Charles Laughton and Ray Milland), *Road to Rio* (1947), and *Dream Girl* (1947).

He served again during the Korean War, attached to the 1st Marine Division from November 1948 to 10 May 1951. This division was in Korea during that conflict and took part in the Inchon landing; Van Brunt was assigned to the Intelligence Department (S-2).

In July 1951 he was transferred to Headquarters Battalion, Marine Corps Station, Quantico, where he served as an instructor, with additional duties at the Marine Corps Education Center. By 4 January 1952 he had again been transferred, and he was company commander of 1st Weapons Company, 3d Battalion, 1st Infantry Training Regiment, Camp J. H. Pendleton. Released from active-duty status in April 1952, he stayed in the Reserves until 1959, when he was detached from the 8th Marine Corps District, New Orleans.

For his service in World War II and the Korean conflict, Van Brunt was decorated with the Silver Star, Bronze Star, American Defense Service Medal, Asiatic-Pacific Area Campaign Medal, World War II Victory Medal, Korean Service Medal, United Nations Service Medal, and the Presidential Unit Citation.

Twice married, after his years in the Corps Van Brunt worked in radio advertising and as Pepsi Cola's representative in Tokyo. He had increasing problems with controlling his alcohol intake, particularly in the 1970s, when he stopped working while living in Honolulu. He commented to a fellow World War II Marine, "it's time to take off the pack." While his second wife ran a travel agency, Van Brunt found too much pleasure in the many bars along the beach, or often, right at home in their apartment on the water. Tad Van Brunt died in 1977 and rests in Honolulu's military veterans' cemetery.

Learning Japanese

Before World War II, when relations were still relatively calm between Japan and the United States, just one Marine Corps officer, an assistant naval attaché in Tokyo, and a few regular Navy officer language students were learning Japanese. From 1939 to 1941, two Marine officers were given this assignment. Two more students were added in December 1941, to help unravel Japanese naval communications. These personnel were the only regulars in the Marine Corps who had Japanese-language qualifications.

During World War II, in response to an alarming shortage of interpreters in the Pacific, about 1,500 reservists were brought into the naval service and trained as Japanese-language officers, including 150 Marines, 70 Waves, and 20 Navy regulars. In addition, 150 Marine Corps enlisted personnel were trained at language schools at Camp Elliott, Camp Lejeune, and other schools set up by line organizations in the field. Their mission was to provide an elementary understanding of Japanese and the ability to communicate in a basic military vocabulary.

The field courses existed for the most part only because of the language officers who wanted to keep their skills, along with enlisted Marines who wanted to learn. A few line officers learned some Japanese, and some who were talented in languages helped to handle moving the prisoners of war.

Camp Elliott's Japanese Language School was started in July 1942. Classes of about twenty-five began each month, lasting for thirteen weeks. The aim was to qualify enlisted men as assistants to language officers; to teach them to handle preliminary questioning of lower-echelon Japanese prisoners, in the hopes of obtaining information that could be useful in the immediate combat situation; and to translate field orders.

Japanese Americans were not accepted into the Marines, due to the pervasive racism and paranoia of the times that was also responsible for interning in U.S. detention camps families who had lived in the United States for decades and considered it their home. (After the war, understandably, some of these citizens opted instead for Japan.)

However, Japanese Americans did account for the main portion of the U.S. Army's language capabilities in the Pacific. In combat operations, Army teams—usually an officer and about ten enlisted nisei—augmented the Marine language sections.

Marine linguists were generally considered to be intelligence personnel. Their chief duties were translating captured documents, interrogating prisoners of war and civilians, identifying enemy equipment, authorizing the release of souvenirs, and, sometimes, transcribing, translating, and interpreting intercepted tactical communcations. Marine commanders were, of course, particularly interested in any intelligence about fortified positions, troop strength, order of battle, and logistic capabilities. Higher authorities had their eye on captured signal code books and reports of airfield site surveys.

During the occupation of Japan, the linguists who accompanied Marine landing forces helped to establish control over parts of Kyushu beyond the beachhead. They also helped with security, and they assisted civil-affairs officers in moving and billeting troops. They were of critical assistance in backing public-information programs, liaising with Japanese authorities, and handling all types of interactions with the Japanese people.

Jonathan Winters

Until age seven, improvisation genius Jonathan Harshman Winters III (born 11 November 1925 in Dayton, Ohio) was raised in the comfortable home of Jonathan Harshman and Alice Kilgore (Rodgers) Winters. An only child, he entertained himself by creating his own sound effects for imagined scenarios using his toys. He made up the people, too, playing a doctor, Robin Hood, an Indian, and many, many others. Later in life, these would evolve into his famous Grandma Maudie Frickert, schoolteacher George Washington, Yale man Binky Bixford, an anonymous Civil War soldier, airline pilot, or truck driver . . . no one could ad-lib with as much wit and speed as the man of a thousand faces and noises, one of America's funniest comedians.

Alice and Jonathan divorced when their son was seven, largely

(Photofest)

because of his father's alcoholism—the Yale graduate, whose forte was math, later did stop drinking. Alice kept things running by herself, moving from their large house into a small apartment. She found work in a factory, kept that until she moved on to a job for a magazine, and eventually got her own interview program on the radio.

As for her young son, his eccentric paternal grandfather became his main companion. Former owner of the Winters National Bank in Dayton, Grandpa Winters loved nothing more than to play pranks and act out imagined situations, and he had no trouble getting his equally fantasy-prone grandson to join him. Together they took on Yellowstone National Park, staying in a first-class hotel, where Winters would return after the war to work briefly in the kitchen.

Jonathan disliked high school and did poorly, anxious to get on with what he imagined to be real life. Greatly influenced by watching his favorite actors do battle in the French Foreign Legion or the U.S. Marines, by age seventeen he could no longer bear it. He quit Dayton High School and enlisted in the U.S. Marine Corps Reserve on 20 October 1943 in Cincinnati.

In January 1944 Jonathan Winters went through boot camp at Parris Island, but then, because of a kidney disease he'd developed, he was laid up for several months in the naval hospital at Philadelphia. Lying alongside men who had suffered severe war wounds was a sobering experience for the budding comedian, who began to see a deep connection between humor and tragedy.

After being released from sick bay, Private Winters was sent to Sea School in Portsmouth, Virginia, and then ordered to the Marine Detachment aboard the battleship USS *Wisconsin,* operating out of Norfolk. Winters was on board for just two months, during which the ship underwent sea trials and initial training in the Chesapeake Bay before being ordered to the Pacific.

On 23 October 1944, at Norfolk, Pfc. Jonathan Winters joined the Marine Detachment of the second U.S. ship to be named *Bon Homme Richard,* the aircraft carrier CV-31. The ship had been launched on 29 April 1944 by the New York Navy Yard and commissioned on 26 November, with Winters aboard. In March 1945, the carrier departed Norfolk for Pacific duty.

After a short training period in Hawaiian waters, in June the "Bonnie Dick" joined Task Group 38.4 off Okinawa. Under the command of Rear Adm. A. W. Radford, the task group consisted of three *Essex*-class carriers and two light carriers (CVLs), Adm. William Frederick "Bull" Halsey's flagship (the battleship *Missouri*), a cruiser, and a destroyer screen.

Leaving Leyte on 1 July with Carrier Air Group (Night) 91 aboard, the *Bon Homme Richard* operated against the Japanese homeland as a night carrier. From 10 July 1945 to the end of the war on 15 August 1945, Jonathan Winters's ship participated in a series of air strikes and surface bombardments against airfields and industrial installations, including in the Tokyo environs, Kyushu, Honshu, Hokkaido, Shikoku, and the Yokosuka Naval Base. As the second atomic bomb was dropped on Nagasaki and Russia declared war on Japan (9 August), the *Bon Homme Richard* detached Task Unit 34.8.1, which bombed Kamaishi. The next day, Japan opened peace negotiations.

Winters was assigned as a light-antiaircraft-gun crewman. Though his ship was not hit by enemy air strikes or kamikaze attacks during this final phase of the Pacific War, she did send up a hail of fire, along with other ships in the unit, when enemy aircraft broke through their combat air patrols.

Winters and his shipmates slept over the bomb-storage magazine, wondering if this would be the night when they would take a hit and reflecting on their sleeping arrangements. One time a kamikaze almost succeeded—but the ship was just grazed. Despite sleeping on top of the bombs, Winters liked knowing that no matter what happened, he and his fellow Marines were in this together, all the way. For the first time in his life, he felt a great sense of camaraderie with his peers, whom he entertained regularly with his side-splitting antics.

When the occupation forces of the Third Fleet Landing Force landed at Yokosuka Naval Base and Yokosuka Air Station in Tokyo, Winters was among them. From 30 August to 6 September 1945, he helped to ensure that the base was secure. He departed his ship on 31 October 1945 and proceeded to Casual Company No. 2 at Treasure Island, San Francisco, then was ordered to the 1st Guard Company at the Marine Barracks, Navy Yard, Philadelphia.

Winters was assigned to the Casual Company at the yard before being honorably discharged as a corporal on 1 March 1946. He was

U.S. Marine carrier detachment exercises 20mm batteries in the Pacific, 1945. (U.S. Navy)

entitled to wear the American Area Campaign Medal, the Asiatic-Pacific Area Campaign Medal with one bronze star, the Navy Occupation Service Medal with Asia clasp, and the World War II Victory Medal.

After finishing high school, he traveled around the country taking odd jobs, including apricot picking, to make ends meet. He briefly attended Kenyon College in Gambier, Ohio, and in 1947 he enrolled at the Dayton Art Institute from which he graduated with a bachelor's of fine arts in 1950. It was here that he met Eileen Ann Schauder, whom he married in 1948. Eileen soon realized that his nonstop hilarious performances should take place before more than her eyes only.

With her encouragement, Winters entered a local humor contest, winning a first-prize wristwatch. Dayton radio station WING staffers were so impressed that in 1949 they hired him as their zaniest disc jockey. In 1950 he went on to WBNS-TV in Columbus, Ohio, for a three-year romp. He then bounced cheerfully into New York City with less than sixty dollars in his pocket.

First appearing at the Blue Angel nightclub, Winters quickly attracted a following and the attention of media personalities. He was invited for guest appearances on the *Mike and Buff Show* (hosted by Mike Wallace and actress Buff Cobb Wallace) and on Arthur Godfrey's *Talent Scouts* program.

But his biggest fan, and most likely the one who assured his stardom, was Jack Paar, who in 1954 introduced him to national audiences on *The Morning Show* on CBS-TV. Appearances on the Steve Allen and Garry Moore shows came next, and in 1956, NBC-TV signed him for a fifteen-minute weekly program, *The Jonathan Winters TV Show,* which enjoyed popularity—but not enough for the star to quit his other work. Winters continued his guest spots on Paar's and Allen's shows, and in early 1958, he filled in for Paar for a two-week run on the *Tonight* show that increased his fame nationwide.

Winters kept pace with a hectic television schedule as well as the nightclub circuit, fueled by cigarette smoking and Scotch drinking. It all proved to be too much, and by 1959 the funny man had run himself into the ground (even though he would have preferred to blast off into the sky with his family, to explore the purer wonders of the cosmos). He suffered a nervous breakdown, and Eileen took him to a private sanatorium. Refusing the doctors' recommendation for shock treatments, he pursued his own therapy and took a hard look at his life. Having seen the other side—fear, death, and loneliness—he treasured the important things all the more.

Basing himself firmly at home with his family, he went fishing with his son on the Long Island Sound, and he painted more than ever. He wrote stories, verse, and song lyrics, and he produced comics, including for the *Saturday Evening Post.* He made clay sculptures. He and Eileen encouraged both their children not only to dare to be different —even slightly strange—but also to revel in it.

For work, he focused on television appearances and dramatic roles, giving up the grueling road performances. He wanted to begin making movies, and in 1961 he appeared in *Alakazam the Great,* followed by *It's a Mad, Mad, Mad, Mad World* (1963). Moving the family to Hollywood, he focused his efforts on appearing in many more films, including *The Loved One* (1965); *The Russians Are Coming, The Russians Are Coming* (1966); *Viva Max* (1969); *The Fish That Saved*

Pittsburgh (1979); and *Moon Over Parador* (1988). His television work has included *The Andy Williams Show* (1965–67; 1970–71), *The Jonathan Winters Show* (1956–57; 1967–69), *The Wacky World of Jonathan Winters* (1972–74), and *Hee-Haw* (1983). He played Robin Williams's son in the series *Mork and Mindy* (1978–82); and Randy Quaid's father, a retired Marine gunnery sergeant, in *Davis Rules* (1991–92), winning an Emmy.

Outside of his professional life, the highly individualistic, completely inimitable Winters has continued to eschew public life and most see-and-be-seen events, in favor of his simpler but richer pursuits at home. In 1979, he did pay a visit to the Marine Corps Recruit Depot in San Diego. While visiting the facility, he said to a Corps newsletter (*CheVron*, March 1979) reporter, "I was always proud of being a Marine. I still won't hesitate to defend it against anyone who talks down about it. I always wanted to march into combat wearing full dress blues. I might have gotten my clock cleaned, but I would have looked good."

Today Winters rarely makes appearances; occasionally he shows up in a commercial. He and Eileen, married for fifty years, live in California. In 1965 he published *Mouse Breath, Social Conformity, and Other Ills* (Bobbs-Merrill), which he wrote and illustrated himself. Since then he has published *Winters' Tales: Stories and Observations for the Unusual* (Random House, 1987) and *Hang-Ups: Paintings by Jonathan Winters* (Random House, 1988). Winters also continues to paint, draw, sculpt, and fish, and he collects Civil War mementos and coins.

A Few More Good Men

Some of the many other actors who served in the Marine Corps include:

Don Adams
Paul Benedict
Harry Blyden
Joseph Bologna
Hugh Brannum
Drew Carey
Philip Carey
Patrick Curtis
R. Lee Ermey
Mike Farrell
Pat Flaherty
Glenn Ford
Clu Galager
Christopher George
Scott Glenn
Lloyd Haynes
Bob Keeshan
John Kellogg
Dan Lauria
Harvey Lembeck
Tim Matheson
John Miljan
Michael Murphy
Warren Oates
Pat Paulsen
Felton Perry
Hari Rhodes

Richard Schall
Raymond Serra
Bo Svenson
Ralph Waite
Dennis Waters
Robert Webber
James Whitmore
Larry Wilcox
Burt Young

Glenn Ford enlisted in the Marines in 1943 and served as a photographic specialist. He joined the Naval Reserve in 1958, serving as a public-affairs naval officer in Vietnam in 1967. (See our chapter in *Stars in Blue*, Naval Institute Press, 1997.)

Lillian Russell and Women in the Marines

With our apologies to any Marines who were (or are) also actresses, we found only renowned stage actress and singer Lillian Russell who fit the bill—almost. Russell starred in four movies: a 1912 film of unknown title, made by Lubin Motion Picture Company; *How to Live 100 Years* (1913); *Wildfire* (1915); and *The Daughters of Two Famous Women* (1931). She was made an honorary noncommissioned Marine officer during World War I for recruiting purposes, a patriotic responsibility that she fulfilled with enthusiasm and imagination.

Russell was born as Helen "Nellie" Louise Leonard, in the Mississippi River town of Clinton, Iowa, on 4 December 1860. Her father, Charles Egbert Leonard, was a newspaperman who founded Clinton's first paper; his wife, Cynthia Hicks Van Name Leonard, helped establish the first Soldiers' Home in Iowa. Nellie was raised in a household that took civic duties and cultural activities seriously.

After making her stage debut at age ten in a school play, Nellie's mind was made up. She felt even more strongly after seeing her first opera, *Mignon*: she would become a singer and perform onstage. She was given voice lessons as an adolescent, and at age eighteen she moved with her mother and a sister to New York, where she continued her vocal training.

Less than a year later, she appeared in the chorus of Edward E. Rice's production of *H.M.S. Pinafore* at the Brooklyn Academy of Music. Lillian Russell was on her way, especially after the dean of vaudeville, Antonio "Tony" Pastor, hired her to appear on Broadway.

Specializing in comic-opera roles, Russell reigned on the American stage until 1919. Beautiful, charming, witty, intelligent, talented, and caring, she was also a significant influence in the political arena. During World War I, determined to do her part for her country, she offered her services to the military to help out however she could. She received an honorary noncommissioned-officer rating of sergeant, and she was sent to work recruiting for the Marines.

She also gave morale-boosting speeches to those who were already in the Corps; she spoke at Quantico and in halls and theaters, on street platforms and in troops' quarters. She sold Liberty bonds and raised money for the various servicemen's funds. She knitted and assembled "comfort kits" for the "boys over there," and she offered to travel over there to provide entertainment for them.

During the years following the war, Lillian Russell became increasingly involved in politics and in working for her chosen causes. She died in 1922, the mother of one child, several times divorced, and married to Alexander P. Moore at the time of her death. Russell was buried in Allegheny Cemetery, Pittsburgh, with full military honors.

While Lillian Russell made an invaluable contribution to the Marine Corps, many other women joined the Corps during World War I. Opha Mae Johnson was the first in U.S. history, enlisting in Washington, D.C., on 13 August 1918. During the course of the war, a total of 305 women in the Marine Reserve performed clerical duties to "Free a Marine to Fight." But when the war ended, Comdt. George Barnett canceled the women's program and discharged all Marines in it.

As World War II began to drain the nation of its manpower resources, Comdt. Thomas Holcomb approved the establishment of the U.S. Marine Corps Women's Reserve. The program was announced on 13 February 1943, which became the birthday of women Marines. The first enlisted class of 722 women completed training at New York's Hunter College in April 1943, and the first officer class (of seventy-five) completed training at Mount Holyoke College, Massachusetts, about two weeks later. By June 1944, female Reserves accounted for 85 percent of enlisted personnel at Headquarters Marine Corps.

After the war the Corps again wanted to disestablish the Women's Reserve, but by this time it was clear that there was a place for women. Additionally, in the event they were ever needed again, it would be easier not to have to start all over again with their training. In 1946 Comdt. Alexander A. Vandegrift allowed the retention of one hun-

In World War I, Recruiting Sergeant Lillian Russell, USMC, gave morale-boosting speeches to those already in the service, raised money for their various funds, and assembled "comfort kits" for the "boys over there."

dred, then three hundred women in the Women's Reserve. No more than one hundred could be kept on active duty at any given time.

In June 1948, President Truman signed legislation allowing women to serve in the Regular military services for the first time: Public Law 625, the Women's Armed Services Integration Act. Females were to account for no more than 2 percent of the Regular forces, but they would have unlimited admission to the Reserves. No woman could serve in combat, in a Navy ship (except for hospital ships and transports), or in aircraft.

The Marine Corps was the last of the services to admit women into its ranks. Col. Katherine A. Towle, who had previously been the second director of the Women's Reserve, was reactivated, accepted a Regular commission, and became the first director of Women Marines in November 1948. On 10 November 1948, eight enlisted female Marines were sworn in. In February 1949, they began recruit training at Parris Island, and that summer, Quantico offered the first Women Officers' Training Class. Of the sixty-seven candidates who began the training, thirty-four made it through the course and were commissioned, seven of them recommended for Regular commissions.

African American women enlisted in the Corps for the first time in mid-1949. Even though male Marines were still segregated, Platoon 7 of the 3d Recruit Training Battalion, Parris Island, became one of the Corps's first integrated units. The third African American woman to join Platoon 7 was Annie L. Grimes, who later became the first black officer to retire from the Corps after twenty years of service.

During the Korean War, female Reserves were mobilized for the first time. As increasing numbers of women joined the Corps, their duties began to expand. From clerical work they found their way into other fields and specialties, including photography, weapons repair, and truck driving. By the end of the Korean War, women in the Marines numbered 2,787.

That total had dropped to 1,448 by 1964, but by 1969, during the Vietnam War, it had again risen to 2,780. Enlisted women were attending advanced schools and were enrolled in the Marine Corps Command and Staff College, and in 1970, the Armed Forces Staff College in Norfolk, Virginia, also opened its doors to women.

Separate branches of the Corps for men and women were done away with in June 1977, and Comdt. Robert H. Barrow sent out the following message to the Marine force in 1980: "Women Marines and male Marines serve side by side in our ranks. They are equal in every sense. They are Marines. They deserve nothing less than outstanding leadership, equal treatment, and equal opportunity for professional development."

The Gulf War became a turning point, not only for the 2,276

females who served in the Marines overseas, but also for those who followed them into the Marines—by the war's end, 9,300 women were Regulars. Four female communicators with the 11th Marines went through the breach on G-Day of Desert Storm; they entered Kuwait, came under hostile fire, and earned the Combat Action Medal. Women served in intelligence, gathering information inside Kuwait on enemy tactical material and command bunkers; they drove trucks through the breach, bringing back prisoners.

By the end of the Gulf War, women were accepted in more occupational categories than ever before, and by 1993, Marine second lieutenant Sarah Deal became the first female to begin training as a naval aviator. She received her wings in 1995.

In 1997, 4.3 percent of all Marine officers were women, and women made up 5.1 percent of the Corps's active-duty enlisted personnel. Most occupational fields (93 percent) were open to women, and 62 percent of all positions were available to them—including combat training. And they were deploying shipboard.

APPENDIX C

The Swinging Sounds of Bob Crosby's Bands

World War II was a long, often vicious struggle that sent American service men and women to all parts of the world. They endured fierce battles on land, at sea, and in the air, and many spent years away from home and their loved ones. Morale was a critical factor during the war, and every effort was made to ensure that military personnel were provided with moments that could distract them from the perils they faced. USO entertainers brought both comic and dramatic relief to those who sat in jungle mud and heat, or in frigid European winters. If only for a while, they provided a diversion for the combat-weary, who could relax for a bit and picture themselves back home.

Service newspapers and radio stations kept the troops informed; pinups adorned lockers and aircraft fuselages. V-mail, a revolutionary process developed by Eastman Kodak, reduced the bulky method of shipping mail by air, thus increasing and expediting the number of letters that reached the "boys and girls" overseas.

Music, too, was a major morale factor during the war. The big-band sound had captivated Americans in the thirties, and some of the best musicians in show business were drafted into the services. Among the most notable bands of the time were the Army's Glenn Miller Orchestra, the Navy's Artie Shaw and Claude Thornhill ensembles, the Coast Guard's Rudy Vallee Orchestra, and Bob Crosby's 5th Marine Division band. The strains of their swing arrangements and romantic interludes served as a magical link between U.S. forces and those they left behind. Nostalgic melodies reminded all that the war would someday be over, and families and loved ones would be reunited.

George Robert "Bob" Crosby was born in Spokane, Washington, on 23 August 1913, the youngest of five sons in the close, musical family that also spawned Bob's older brother, show-business icon Bing

Crosby. Despite the ever-present shadow of his famous brother, Bob Crosby, who also had talent, made it on his own in the musical world, and with noteworthy success. In 1935 he accepted the job of leading a swinging, vibrant, and very popular jazz Dixieland band, which became known as the Bobcats, or the Bob Crosby Band. The highly talented and respected group provided musical thrills for appreciative audiences, who swirled to the beat of the Bobcats' spirited arrangements. After three years of earning percentages of the night's take at clubs and hotels throughout the country—New York, Boston, Los Angeles, Chicago—they got a long run at the Windy City's Black Hawk Club.

Crosby was one of the few bandleaders who did not play an instrument himself. Nor did he sing, though he had sung before, with the Dorsey Brothers band. But his voice was not his strongest suit either. Bob Crosby's special talent lay in acting as the band's front man. Crosby, always unassuming and frank about his level of skill, had a natural grace, charm, and humor, and he knew how to handle a crowd.

He was genuinely supportive of the talent that surrounded him, which included, at various times, brilliant players such as trumpeter Billy Butterfield, pianist Joe Sullivan, trumpeter Charlie Spivak, trombonist Buddy Morrow (Moe Zudekoff), tenor saxist Eddie Miller, clarinetist Matty Matlock, and bass player and arranger Bob Haggart. Singers who passed through included Doris Day, Gloria DeHaven, and Kay Starr; among the arrangers were Henry Mancini, Ray Conniff, Nelson Riddle, and Paul Weston. Competition among the big bands was fierce, and musicians jumped from band to band for pay as well as for personal reasons. But Bob Crosby was the right pick for a band that became one of the best.

In 1939 the Bobcats landed the Camel Caravan radio series and added singer and composer Johnny Mercer to their roster. They continued on their roll, with such hit recordings as "Big Noise from Winnetka" and "South Rampart Street Parade." And the Bobcats were featured in several movies, including *Sis Hopkins* (1941), *Let's Make Music* (1940), *Thousands Cheer* (1943), and *Pardon My Rhythm* (1944).

But, as the war began to take away famed musicians of the big-band era, it was obvious that the end was nigh. Several of Crosby's musicians were drafted, and he was commissioned a second lieutenant in the Marine Corps in 1944. Assigned as band director of the 5th Marine

Marine 2d Lt. Bob Crosby, band director of the 5th Marine Division.

Division, he formed a musical group that traveled throughout the Pacific for fourteen months, entertaining and presenting shows. His duty stations included Headquarters Fleet Marine Forces; Headquarters Company, Headquarters Battalion, 5th Marine Division; Marine Corps Band San Diego; USS *Middleton* (APA-25); Marine Corps Barracks, Naval Operating Base, Terminal Island, San Pedro; Marine Barracks, Treasure Island, San Francisco; 1st Marine Corps District, New York; and Headquarters U.S. Marine Corps, Washington, D.C.

Bob Crosby received his honorable discharge in early 1946 at the rank of second lieutenant, entitled to wear the World War II Victory Medal, American Area Campaign Medal, and Asiatic-Pacific Area Campaign Medal.

Following his discharge, he appeared in the movie *The Singing Sher-*

Crosby and his band play for resting troops at Falalop, Ulithi, 1944.

iff (1946) and formed a new band, which toured the West Coast play-ing at Army camps. They also regularly played at the Palladium on Sunset Boulevard, home away from home for on-liberty Marines. The Bobcats were back in business, though they never reached the level of popularity they'd attained before the war. Among the band members were now many veterans, including violinist Morris (King) Perelmuler, a former Marine sergeant who had been with the 3d Division's Merry Men. Perelmuler wrote the song "Salute to the Marines," dedicated to Gen. Graves B. Erskine and the 3d Division.

Meanwhile, the lucrative potential of television work had attracted Crosby's notice. He decided to go out on his own, and in the years that followed, he enjoyed success on television and in nightclubs, and he took shows to Honolulu and Australia. He hosted CBS-TV's *Bob Crosby Show*, featuring musical talent such as the vocalist group the

Adm. William F. Halsey, USN, commander of the U.S. Third Fleet, thanks Crosby and the band for a great show, 1944.

Modernaires. From time to time, he got the Bobcats back together for a series of gigs.

In the 1970s, Bob Crosby joined other renowned band leaders, including Frankie Carle, Buddy Morrow, Art Mooney, and Freddy Martin, to tour the States with a group of musicians, reviving the big-band sounds of a past era. But by the end of the seventies, bookings were scarce and the group disbanded. Crosby continued to appear on television and in musical programs.

Other movies in which he appeared include *Kansas City Kitty* (1944), *See Here, Private Hargrove* (1944), *When You're Smiling* (1950), *Two Tickets to Broadway* (1951), *Road to Bali* (1952), *Senior Prom* (1958), and *The Five Pennies* (1959). Bob Crosby died in 1993 at age eighty, leaving five children and seven grandchildren.

Entertaining the Troops

Performer Marion Davies buys tickets from a Marine for their
tobacco fund during World War I.

During the "Great War," actress Mary Pickford *(second from left)* visits with Brig. Gen. Charles L. McCawley, quartermaster, USMC *(left)*; and Mrs. and Maj. Gen. Comdt. George Barnett. (Mr. Thacker)

Actress Ruth Low tries out a Curtiss airplane as Marine recruiters look on, Miami, Florida, 1918.

Joe E. Brown jokes with Marines in Peiping, China, 1934.

Eddie Bracken's USO troupe arrives at Falalop, July 1945, on its way to entertain the troops at Palau.

Peggy Ryan appears in Eddie Bracken's show at Falalop, July 1945.

Marines watch drummer seaman second class Jackie Cooper on Oahu, January 1945.

Gary Cooper gets some chow with Marines in the mess hall during World War II, South Pacific.

Boxing twins Harvey *(left)* and Moe Weiss entertain actresses *(from left)* Mary Elliott, Rosita Moreno, and Frances Fay. Guadalcanal, February 1944.

Randy Scott *(fourth from left)* relaxes with Marines on Guadalcanal, January 1944.

Providing much-needed recreation for Marine, Army, and Navy troops, Ray Bolger (jitterbugging) and pianist/composer Little Jack Little toured the South Pacific with the USO in late 1943. On Guadalcanal, they were also their own stagehands in a nonstop two-hour act.

During World War II, Merle Oberon visited wounded Marines at Mare Island Naval Hospital. (U.S. Navy)

Danny Kaye laughs it up with four thousand 5th Marine Division occupation troops, Sasebo, Japan, in 1946. Across the front of the Seabee-built stage, someone scrawled, "Officers Keep Out: Enlisted Men's Country."

Jane Russell and Bob Hope, backstage with Marines at Camp Pendleton, 1951.

Hollywood celebrities including Jan Sterling *(second from right)* and Paul Douglas *(right)* were with a USO troupe that entertained Leathernecks of the 1st Marine Division in Korea, January 1952.

Singing star Frances Langford and her husband, actor Jon Hall, put on a USO show for the 1st Marine Divison, Korea, 1952.

Movie star Piper Laurie traveled to Korea with Johnny Grant's USO troupe, to the delight of more than three thousand members of the 5th Marines, 1953.

First Marine Division Leathernecks, just a few miles behind the front lines in Korea, 1952, take a break to revel in a few songs personally delivered by Betty Hutton.

Martha Raye is made an hononary Marine upon her arrival at Danag, South Vietnam, for a USO show in 1965.

Marines of the 3d Battalion, 9th Regiment, 3d Marine Division, get an up-close visit with idol John Wayne in Vietnam, 1966.

Charlton Heston spends time in the field with the men of F Company, 2d Battalion, 9th Marine Regiment, in Vietnam, 1966.

Bibliography

Books and Periodicals

The authors gratefully acknowledge the kind permission of Donald Zec and Anthony Fowles to use excerpts from the book *Marvin: The Story of Lee Marvin*.

Alexander, Joseph H. *Utmost Savagery: The Three Days of Tarawa*. Annapolis, Md.: Naval Institute Press, 1995.

Allen, Sgt. Lindley S. "Return of the Taisho" (on Tad Van Brunt). *Leatherneck*, February 1948.

Allis, Tim, and Andrew Abrahams. "Hello . . . Daddy? *Northern Exposure*'s Barry Corbin Finds the Daughter He Never Knew He Had." *People*, 12 October 1992.

Alvarez, Eugene. "The Lone Ranger—Sergeant Lee B. Powell, USMC." *Leatherneck*, July 1987.

Amory, Cleveland. "How Jonathan Winters Turns Pain into Laughter." *Parade*, 20 December 1987.

Applebaum, Ralph. "Flying High" (on George Roy Hill). *Films and Filming*, August 1979.

Arnold, Gary. "Movie Hero Steve McQueen Dies of Heart Attack at Age 50." *Washington Post*, 8 November 1980.

Bailey, Cpl. Gilbert P. "Wake Island Flier—Now a Real Marine" (on Macdonald Carey). Undated USMC press release.

Bartlett, Tom. "Hugh O'Brian and His Youth Foundation." *Leatherneck*, March 1983.

"Bob Burns Dead; Radio Comedian." *New York Times*, 3 February 1956, 23.

Brian Keith obit. *Leatherneck*, September 1997.

Burns, Bob. "How My Bazooka and Me Came Down to Hollywood, or Durned if I Didn't Do It." *Sunday Evening Star*, Kansas City, 14 February 1937.

Carey, Macdonald. *The Days of My Life*. New York: St. Martin's Press, 1991.

Carpenter, Dennis, and Frank Bisogno. *Anyone Here a Marine? Popular Entertainment and the Marines*. Great Neck, N.Y.: Brightlights Publications, 1992.

Chapin, Capt. John C. "Breaching the Marianas: The Battle for Saipan." Washington, D.C.: Marine Corps Historical Center, Pamphlet History series, 1994.

Clark, John. "On the Beach" (on Dale Dye). *Premiere*, June 1998.

Cobbledick, Gordon. "Bill Lundigan on Other End of Movie Camera Filming Bloody Marine Battles on Okinawa." *Post-Standard* (Syracuse, N.Y.), 20 March 1945.

Coffin, Patricia. "Tyrone Power, Pin-Up Boy." *Look*, 3 September 1946, 28.

"Comdr. Glenn Ford," *Philadelphia Inquirer,* 7 February 1967.

Davidson, Bill. "The Entertainer" (on George Roy Hill). *New York Times Magazine,* 16 March 1975.

Demaris, Ovid. "I'm Available: At 70, Glenn Ford's Still Raring to Go." *Parade,* 9 November 1986, 4.

Dillman, Bradford. *Are You Anybody?* Santa Barbara, Calif.: Fithian Press, 1997.

Donati, William. *Ida Lupino.* Lexington: University Press of Kentucky, 1996.

Elias, Justine. "Dreaming Private Ryan" (on Dale Dye). *Us,* August 1998.

Erskine, Col. John C. "Language Officers Recall Combat Roles in the Pacific." *Fortitudine* 15 (Spring 1986): 23.

"Famed Comedian Re-joins Marines as Show Returns" (on Jonathan Winters). *Jacksonville Daily News* (Associated Press), Jacksonville, N.C., 16 December 1991.

"Family Man" (on Brian Keith), *People,* 7 August 1997.

Fine, Marshall. *Harvey Keitel: The Art of Darkness.* New York: Fromm International, 1997.

Frank, Benis M. "Wartime French Allies Honor 'Underground' Marines" (on Peter J. Ortiz). *Fortitudine,* Fall 1994.

"George C. Scott: Tempering a Terrible Fire." *Time,* 22 March 1971, 63.

Guiles, Fred Lawrence. *Tyrone Power: The Last Idol.* New York: Berkley Books, 1980.

Hawkes, Ellen. "The Day His Father Drove Away." *Parade,* 26 February 1989.

Hayden, Sterling. *Wanderer.* London: Longmans, Green, 1964.

"Heavy Star" (on George C. Scott). Show Business column, *Time,* 23 February 1962.

Hewitt, Capt. Linda L. *Women Marines in World War I.* Washington, D.C.: History and Museums Division, Headquarters, U.S. Marine Corps, 1974.

"Hollywood Star, Back from Wars, in Naval Hospital" (on Bill Lundigan). *San Diego Journal,* 7 August 1945.

Hopper, Hedda. "Break for Bill [Lundigan]—at Last!" *Chicago Sunday Tribune,* 14 August 1949.

International News Service. "Capt. Hayward, Tarawa Hero, Leaves Hospital." South Bend *Tribune,* 19 April 1944.

Jarlett, Franklin. *Robert Ryan: A Biography and Critical Filmography.* Jefferson, N.C., and London: McFarland Classics, 1997.

Johnson, Robert, Jr. "An Actor's Life" (on Gerald O'Loughlin). *Leatherneck,* March 1988.

———. "Lee Marvin." *Leatherneck,* July 1986.

"Jonathan Winters Here for All Service Meet." *Quantico Sentry,* 10 June 1980.

"Jonathan Winters 'reenlists,'" Marine Corps *CheVron,* Marine Corps Recruit Depot San Diego, March 1979.

Koenenn, Connie. "Marshaling His Forces for the Future" (on Hugh O'Brian). Life and Style, *Los Angeles Times,* 16 June 1996.

Lambert, Pam, F. X. Feeney, and Carolyn Ramsay. "The War That Was" (on Jonathan Winters). *People,* 7 August 1995.

LaPointe, Lt. Cpl. Thomas J. "Medals Awarded to Actor Brian Keith During Ceremony." *Leatherneck,* September 1988.

Laurent, Lawrence. "Quick Wit of Winters Can Make Paar's Show." *Washington Post*, 5 August 1960.

Lawliss, Chuck. *The Marine Book: A Portrait of America's Military Elite*. New York: Thames and Hudson, 1992.

Lear, Martha Weiman. "Winging It with Jonathan Winters." *New York Times Magazine*, 28 March 1963.

"Lee Powell, Lone Ranger of Movies, Killed in Action." Associated Press Release, 31 August 1944.

Legge, Steven J. "U.S. Marine Colonel Peter Ortiz Served Covertly with the Resistance in France." *World War II*, July 1998.

Lewis, Jack. "Colt, Mare's Leg, and Derringer: Three Former Marines Went Thataway to Fame and Fortune on TV" (on Jock Mahoney, Steve McQueen, and John Russell). *Leatherneck*, July 1960.

Lombardi, John. "Scenes from a Bad Movie Marriage" (on Harvey Keitel). *New York*, 12 January 1998.

"Louis Hayward, 75, Swashbuckling Hero in Adventure Films." *New York Times*, 23 February 1985.

Marvin, Pamela. *Lee: A Romance*. London: Faber and Faber, 1997.

Mattingly, Robert E. "Who Knew Not Fear" (on Peter J. Ortiz). The Colonel Robert D. Heinl Jr. 1983 Memorial Award in Marine Corps History. Washington, D.C.: History and Museums Division, Headquarters, U.S. Marine Corps, 1983.

McGrady, Mike. "Hackman, Hollywood's Hardworking Star." *Newsday*, 22 February 1987.

McMahon, Ed, and Carroll Carroll. *Here's Ed: or How to Be a Second Banana, from Midway to Midnight*. New York: G. P. Putnam's Sons, 1976.

Morison, Samuel Eliot. *History of the United States Naval Operations in World War II*, 15 vols. Boston: Little, Brown, 1947–1962.

Moseley, Virginia Kleitz. "*Sting* Director a Rare Hollywood Bird" (on George Roy Hill). Los Angeles *Herald-Examiner*, 7 April 1974.

Moskin, J. Robert. *The U.S. Marine Corps Story*. New York: Little, Brown, 1992.

Mothner, Ira. "George C. Scott: Don Quixote on Broadway." *Look*, 6 November 1962, 87.

Myers, Sgt. Robert H. USMC. "A Marine's Best Friend Is His Bazooka" (on Bob Burns). *Leatherneck*, June 1944.

Newsclip from the *Houston Chronicle* on Ed McMahon. 24 February 1982.

Nolan, William F. *McQueen*. New York: Congdon and Weed, 1984.

Norman, Michael. "Drillmasters' Seminar: The Art of War" (on Dale Dye). *New York Times*, 4 February 1990.

O'Neill, William J. "The Derring-Do of Peter Ortiz." *Marine Corps League*, Autumn 1992.

Parsons, Louella O. "Ida Lupino Admits Rift with Captain Louis Hayward." Los Angeles *Examiner*, 21 July 1944.

Potter, E. B. *Sea Power: A Naval History*. Annapolis, Md.: Naval Institute Press, 1981.

Price, George Ward. "In Bivouac with the Legion." In *In Morocco with the Legion* (on Peter Ortiz). London: Jarrolds, 1934.

Ray, Donald, and Anne Bowbeer. *Lillian Russell.* Westport, Conn.: Greenwood, 1997.

Riblett, Pfc. Leonard. "Back to the Bobcats" (on Bob Crosby). *Leatherneck,* July 1946.

"A 'Risk Actor' Cuts Loose" (on George C. Scott). *Life,* 8 March 1968.

Schumach, Murray. "'Off Broadway' Urged for Films" (on George Roy Hill). *New York Times,* 6 April 1962.

Settel, Irving. "A Pictorial History of Radio." New York: Grosset and Dunlap, 1967.

Simon, George T. "Bob Crosby." In *The Big Bands.* New York: Schirmer Books, 1981.

St. Johns, Adela Rogers. "Return of the Marine" (on Tyrone Power). *Photoplay,* May 1946, 32.

Suid, Lawrence H. "Marines in the Movies." In *The Marines,* edited by Edwin Howard Simmons and J. Robert Moskin. Quantico, Va.: Marine Corps Heritage Foundation, 1998.

Tayman, John, and Kristina Johnson. "The Doctor Is In (Again)" (on Macdonald Carey). *People,* 16 December 1991.

Thackrey, Ted. "Actor William Lundigan Dies; Began Career in 1937." *Los Angeles Times,* 22 December 1975.

———. "Film, TV Actor Louis Hayward Dies." *Los Angeles Times,* 22 February 1985.

"That Irishman" (on Bill Lundigan). *Photoplay,* May 1950.

Toffell, Neile McQueen. *My Husband, My Friend.* New York: Atheneum, 1986.

Vergun, Gy. Sgt. David. "Brian Keith." *Marines,* November 1992.

Viets, Pat. "Colonel Ortiz: Marine Hero Who Lived Adventurous Life Full of Cloak-and-Dagger Thrillers." *Marines,* July 1988.

Washington Post, 8 January 1967. UPI photos and captions covering Glenn Ford's thirty-day tour of duty in the Naval Reserves.

Waxman, Sharon. "The Scoundrel King" (on Gene Hackman). *Washington Post,* 6 October 1996.

Wheeler, Richard. *A Special Valor.* Edison, N.J.: Castle Books, 1996.

White, W. V. H. "Harvey Keitel: Actor, Producer, Marine." *Leatherneck,* June 1996.

Wilson, Earl. "Meet Hugh O'Brian, Parachutist." *New York Post,* 12 October 1965.

"Winging It" (on Jonathan Winters). *Newsweek,* 18 May 1964.

Zec, Donald. *Marvin: The Story of Lee Marvin.* New York: St. Martin's Press, 1980.

Selected Reference Books

Aaker, Everett. *Television Western Players of the Fifties: A Biographical Encyclopedia of All Regular Cast Members in Western Series, 1949–1959.* Jefferson, N.C., and London: MacFarland and Company, 1997.

Current Biography Yearbook. New York: H. W. Wilson Company, 1941 through 1996.

Halliwell, Leslie. *Halliwell's Film Guide: 1996, Revised and Updated,* John Walker, ed. New York: HarperPerennial, 1995.

Katz, Ephraim. *The Film Encyclopedia.* New York: Harper Collins Publishers, Inc., 1994.

Law, Jonathan, ed. *Brewer's Cinema: A Phrase and Fable Dictionary.* London: Market House Books, 1995.

Maltin, Leonard. *Movie Encyclopedia.* New York: Penguin Books, 1994.

———. *1996 Movie and Video Guide.* New York: Penguin Books, 1995.

Nash, J. Robert, and Stanley Ralph and Ross. *Movies: The Motion Picture Guide* (and annual vols. through 1997). Chicago: Cinebooks, 1987.

Newcomb, Horace, ed. *Museum of Broadcast Communications Encyclopedia of Television.* Chicago and London: Fitzroy Dearborn Publishers, 1997.

Parish, James Robert, and Vincent Terrace. *The Complete Actors' Television Credits, 1948–1988,* 2d ed. Vol. 1, *Actors.* Metuchen, N.J., and London: Scarecrow Press, 1989.

Quinlan, David. *Quinlan's Illustrated Directory of Film Stars,* 3d ed. London: B. T. Batsford, 1991.

Thomas, Nicholas, ed. *International Dictionary of Films and Filmmakers.* Vol. 3, *Actors and Actresses.* Detroit and London: St. James Press, 1992.

Variety Obituaries. New York and London: Garland Publishing.

Correspondence and Interviews (all with Jim Wise)

Corbin, Barry: 1998.
Dillman, Bradford: 1998.
Dye, Dale: 1998.
Hayden, Catherine (widow of Sterling Hayden): 1997.
Hatch, Norman T., former Marine staff sergeant (and retired major) and member of Second Marine Division Tarawa Photographic Section, under Capt. Louis Hayward, 1998.
LaSalle, Robert (on Peter Ortiz): 1998.
Nelson, Glenn, WWII Japanese Language Officer, 29th Marines, 6th Marine Division, on Okinawa (on Tad Van Brunt): 1998.
O'Brian, Hugh: 1997.
O'Loughlin, Gerald S.: 1997.
Ortiz, Jean (widow of Peter Ortiz): 1998.
Risler, Jack (on Peter Ortiz): 1998.
Slaughter, Glen, WWII Japanese Language Officer, 29th Marines, 6th Marine Division, on Okinawa (on Tad Van Brunt): 1998.

Official Records and Archival Sources

Marine Corps Historical Center, Washington, D.C. USMC press releases, action reports, unit histories, miscellaneous reports, citations, and other official documents, including the following:
Hamilton, John. Documentation including citation of Silver Star: notification of Yugoslavia's awarding Order of Merit to Hayden; copy of court docu-

ment changing Sterling and Madeleine Hayden's last name to Hamilton, 25 June 1943.

"Marine Air Warning Squadron Three/Unit History" (on Macdonald Carey).

"Provisional Marine Landing Force Battalion Orders, USS *Bon Homme Richard* (CV-31)," 19 August 1945.

Service records, press clips, and biographical information on numerous actors, including Bob Burns, Brian Keith, Steve McQueen, Hugh O'Brian, Peter Ortiz, Tyrone Power, John Russell, and Jonathan Winters.

"United States Marine Corps Lineage of Headquarters Battalion, 3rd Marine Division," 14 February 1997.

"United States Marine Corps Lineage of 12th Marines," 7 November 1997.

National Personnel Records Center, St. Louis, Missouri. Military records of numerous actors (released under Freedom of Information Act), including Barry Corbin, Brian Marion Dennehy, 1st Lt. Bradford Dillman, Eugene Alden Hackman, John Hamilton (Sterling Hayden), Charles L. Hayward, Cpl. William Paul Lundigan, Steve McQueen, George W. Peppard, Lee B. Powell, George C. Scott, Frederick Baskerville Van Brunt, and Jonathan Harshman Winters III.

National Archives, College Park, Maryland. Official documentation and action reports, such as "Strikes Against Hokkaido, Honshu, Kyushu, and Shikoku," USS *Bon Homme Richard* (CB-31) action report, 2 July–15 August 1945.

Navy Department press and radio news releases, such as "Marine Combat Photographers in First Waves at Tarawa to Get Picture Story" (on Louis Hayward), 4 December 1943.

Whitlow, Capt. Robert H., USMCR. *U.S. Marines in Vietnam: The Advisory and Combat Assistance Era, 1954–1964*. Washington, D.C.: History and Museums Division, Headquarters, U.S. Marine Corps, 1977.

Other Sources

Academy of Motion Picture Arts and Sciences Library, Los Angeles. Biographical and other information about many actors, including Louis Hayward (Metro-Goldwyn-Mayer biography, 14 March 1935) and William Lundigan (United Artists biography, 15 August 1966).

Don Fedderson Productions, Studio City, California. Biography of Brian Keith, 1966.

Margaret Herrick Library, Center for Motion Picture Study, Academy of Motion Picture Arts and Sciences, Academy Foundation, Beverly Hills. Biographical information and newsclips on Tad Van Brunt.

Miscellaneous copies of official certificates and citations and other service documentation, sent to authors by Marines or their families.

Miscellaneous copies of studio press releases and biographies.

Index

About the Authors

Capt. James E. Wise, Jr., USN (Ret.) is the author or coauthor of several books, including *Stars in Blue* (Naval Institute Press, 1997) and *Sailors' Journey into War* (with Robert Maher, Kent State University Press, 1998). He has also published many historical articles in naval and maritime journals and is currently working on a third book for the "stars" series, *Stars in Khaki.* Captain Wise lives in Alexandria, Virginia.

Anne Collier Rehill, who has worked in publishing for many years, coauthored *Stars in Blue* with Captain Wise and has written numerous articles for periodicals. She currently resides in State College, Pennsylvania, where she teaches English at Penn State University and continues her writing.